THE MARSHALL CAVENDISH
☆ ☆ ☆ ILLUSTRATED ☆ ☆ ☆
ENCYCLOPEDIA OF
WORLD WAR II

VOLUME 14

THE MARSHALL CAVENDISH
☆ ☆ ☆ ILLUSTRATED ☆ ☆ ☆
ENCYCLOPEDIA OF
WORLD WAR II

Based on the original text by
Lieutenant Colonel Eddy Bauer

CONSULTANT EDITOR

Brigadier General James L. Collins, Jr., U.S.A.
CHIEF OF MILITARY HISTORY,
DEPARTMENT OF THE ARMY

MARSHALL CAVENDISH CORPORATION/NEW YORK

CONTENTS

Editorial Director: Brian Innes
Editor-in-chief; Brigadier Peter Young, D.S.O., M.C., M.A.
Managing Editor: Richard Humble
Editor: Christopher Chant
Art Editor: Jim Bridge

© Orbis Publishing Limited 1972
© Éditions Alphée, Monaco 1966
Library of Congress Catalog No. 72-95429
Printed in Great Britain

GENERAL DE GAULLE
and the Fighting French

△ De Gaulle inspecting troops in Britain.
◁ "The French Army in combat" by Raoul Auger. For thousands of Frenchmen, de Gaulle's status as the figurehead of French resistance remained inviolate.

1. *Exultant French submariners wave and cheer in Algiers after their dramatic dash from Toulon in 1940.*
2. *With the Free French Navy. General de Gaulle, followed by Admiral Muselier, visits the Free French sloop* La Moqueuse.

De Gaulle's counterblast to Pétain's acceptance of France's defeat in 1940 kept the spirit of French resistance alive, but for a considerable period he had no armies with which to fight. The colonial troops which escaped the disaster in France remained subject to the Vichy régime, and de Gaulle was accordingly obliged to start virtually from scratch – but the men who rallied to the Cross of Lorraine – the symbol of "Free France" – gave him splendid material with which to work towards the rehabilitation of France's honour.

They had a vivid sense of mission. They were ardent patriots. And their desire to hit back and eventually fight their way home made them formidable soldiers.

But de Gaulle had airmen and sailors as well. The former included the Free French "Alsace" Squadron which operated from Biggin Hill and took part in fighter sweeps over their country. Their ranks produced Pierre Clostermann, who ended up commanding a fighter wing in the R.A.F. and wrote *The Big Show*, one of the best books to come out of World War II, which gives a

vivid picture of the life of a fighter pilot. And the Free French Navy was built up from ships which escaped to Britain in 1940: the old battleship *Courbet*, the submarines *Rubis* and *Surcouf*, the destroyers *Le Triomphant* and *Leopard*, and the sloops *Commandant Duboc*, *Commandant Domine*, *La Moqueuse*, *Chevreuil*, and *Savorgnan de Brazza*. Vice-Admiral Muselier, who escaped from Marseilles aboard a British collier and reached England via Gibraltar, was the commander of the Free French Navy. He proved a worthy colleague of de Gaulle.

For the Free French soldiers, the first major turning-point came with the battle of Gazala in May-June 1942. There the Free French troops under General Koenig held the Bir Hakeim box, the southernmost extremity of the 8th Army's defensive front, around which Rommel threw his great encircling move into the rear areas of 8th Army. The Bir Hakeim garrison, completely surrounded, held out from May 27 until June 10, beating off repeated attacks and enduring massive Stuka bombardment, and finally

4

3. *De Gaulle with Air Chief-Marshal Leigh-Mallory after visiting Free French pilots serving with the R.A.F., in 1941.*
4. *Shortly after D-Day: de Gaulle in pensive mood.*

3

5. *De Gaulle decorates Colonel Almikvari of the Foreign Legion with the* Croix de la Libération *after the battle for Bir Hakeim in May-June 1942. Bir Hakeim, the southernmost "box" of the Gazala Line, was superbly defended by its French garrison; and the battle earned the Free French combatant troops the title of "Fighting French".*

6. *Legionnaire officers in Bir Hakeim.*

7. *Men of General Leclerc's desert column in Tunisia after their epic march from Lake Chad.*

8. *A briefing for a pilot flying with the "Normandie Niemen" squadron in Russia. This volunteer unit was originally known as the "Normandie Regiment"; it earned the honorific title "Normandie Niemen" after an air battle during the fighting on the East Prussia frontier in October 1944, when 26 German planes were downed by the French pilots with no loss to themselves.*

9. *Triumphant return. Back on French soil after D-Day, de Gaulle addresses an enthusiastic crowd in Bayeux, Normandy.*

breaking out through the German ring. It was this exploit which earned the Free French the new title of "Fighting French"; and Bir Hakeim was the first battle honour won by de Gaulle's forces.

Later in the desert war came the epic march of General Leclerc's column from Chad in French Equatorial Africa to join up with the Allied forces advancing against Rommel.

The invasion of Vichy France by the Germans in November 1942 radically changed the situation. The split allegiance–Vichy France versus de Gaulle–was eliminated. But personality clashes caused much tension at the top for a while, particularly between de Gaulle and General Giraud, who escaped from prison in Germany but who had strong ideas of his own on how the Allied High Command should be running the war. (Giraud's personal view was that the "Torch" invasion forces, on entering the Mediterranean, should turn left and invade southern France instead of right to land in North Africa.)

The colonial troops in the ranks of the Fighting French won a splendid reputation for themselves. A highlight came during the final Allied push at Cassino in 1944, where General Juin's *goums* swarmed through the mountains and unseamed the strongest part of the German defence line.

Much ink has been spilled over the pros and cons of the "Dragoon" landing in southern France in August 1944, but one fact at least remains clear. When the "Dragoon" force pushed north

and joined hands with the British and American armies advancing eastwards from Normandy, a French army now stood in the line on equal terms with the other component units of "Overlord". This was the 1st Army, commanded by the dashing General de Lattre de Tassigny. It had much hard fighting to do, most notably in the reduction of the "Colmar Pocket", which bulged into the Allied front line on the western bank of the Rhine. But its presence–let alone its performance–gave France the right to join the other Allies at the table when Germany surrendered in May 1945.

The wheel had come full circle from the disaster of 1940. De Gaulle had set the initial spark. From the survivors of Dunkirk and Narvik there had grown a new and determined fighting force, one totally different from the flabby and demoralised army which had gone to war in September 1939. Under de Gaulle's leadership the Fighting French grew into an efficient and confident entity. It won its own battle honours–Bir Hakeim, Cassino, Colmar. It produced dashing generals of Patton's stamp–Leclerc and de Lattre foremost among them–and its own fighter aces.

It was a superb achievement, although painfully attained. De Gaulle's rigid convictions of his duty to France caused constant clashes with his Allies; but he had saved his country's honour in 1940, and the men who rallied to him and carried on the fight upheld that important honour nobly.

Aid from the Greeks...

The Greek troops who flung the Italians back into Albania and faced the German invasion of April 1940 were magnificent soldiers, and it was a tragedy for the Allied cause in the Mediterranean that no large-scale evacuation could be mounted to include them. There were two obvious reasons for this: the pace of the German advance and the inadequate resources of the British Mediterranean Fleet. But the German conquest of the mainland made no difference to the fighting spirit of the Greek troops on Crete, many of which carried on the fight with the British in the Western Desert.

Here they served with the 8th Army, organised as a brigade. When Montgomery launched his attack at Alamein in October 1942 the Greeks, under Brigadier Katsotas, were held in initial reserve, together with two Fighting French brigades, a Fighting French flying column, and two British armoured brigades.

Unhappily, one of the strongest influences on the Greek soldiers abroad was the civil strife at home. As in Yugoslavia, so in Greece: the Germans were not the sole enemy of the resistance fighters, who as often as not were locked in battle with rival political groups. In Greece the main internal feud was between loyalists and Communists. By the summer of 1944 the Communist-inspired E.A.M. (National Liberation Front) had set up a provisional government in the Greek mountains—one which owed no allegiance to King George II and his government in exile. As a result of the close attention paid to the conflict by the Greek troops abroad, a mutiny in sympathy broke out among the Greek soldiers in Egypt in April 1944, which had to be suppressed by the British authorities.

The liberation of Greece began in October 1944; but the Greek troops which had been serving abroad were given no part in the proceedings. Churchill was determined to head off the possibility of a total Communist takeover in Greece and he insisted that British troops be sent in from Italy.

2

GREECE FIGHTS ON

3

1. and 2. Posters honouring the "fighting Greeks". As at Dunkirk, the British evacuated as many of their Allies as possible when they pulled out of Greece and Crete, and a Greek brigade fought with the 8th Army in the Western Desert.
3. Middle East barbecue: Greek troops prepare for a feast of roast lamb.
4. Hospital cases. Greek army, navy, and air force patients on the road to recovery chat with nurses in a Middle East hospital.

4

...and from the Czechs

After the German occupation of Czechoslovakia in March 1939, there was no lack of attempts by Czech soldiers and airmen to escape to the West and fight again. The escape routes were hazardous and extremely roundabout: south through Rumania to the Middle East. France was the first country to offer assistance for the formation of a Free Czech legion, which was formed at Agde in the south. Recruits trickled in not only from Czechoslovakia but from Palestine, and the French Foreign Legion released Czech soldiers who wished to re-enlist in their own unit.

Two Czech regiments, neither fully trained nor fully equipped, were flung into the Battle of France in June 1940. They were immediately swept up in the disastrous retreat from the Marne and fell back to the south. The British sent transports to Sète and Bordeaux to bring off the Czechs, but three-quarters of them failed to arrive at the embarkation ports in time.

In the United Kingdom the Czechs were re-formed as a brigade. A compromise was found which enabled the unit to liaise smoothly with the British while retaining its own internal organisation. For example, each infantry battalion retained its own pioneer platoon for explosive, demolition, and light bridging work.

As with the Poles, the Soviet Union raised Czech formations to operate with the Red Army. This was considerably helped by the sizeable Czech communities inside the Soviet Union – a convenient source of manpower.

Unlike the Poles, the Czech government-in-exile in London warmly approved of the existence of a Czech formation serving with the Russians. This, which in its early days numbered only about 3,000 men under Colonel Svoboda (later War Minister in the Czech Government in Prague), first saw action in March 1943. The unit scored a signal victory on April 2, for which the Soviet press greatly lauded it. On the 10th, warm congratulations from both members of the government-in-exile and Czech communist deputies in Moscow were received. Captain Jaros, killed in action, was posthumously awarded the title of Hero of the Soviet Union while Svoboda was given the Order of Lenin. Another 82 men of the unit that had so distinguished itself in the fighting around the ancient city of Khar'kov were also decorated by the Soviet military authorities.

As the war progressed, the Czech contingent was raised to corps size and this was in the forefront of the battle during the Slovak rising of August-October 1944, fighting its way across the Carpathians through the Dukla Pass to join hands with the insurgents.

A more static rôle lay in store for the Czech troops in the West. Unlike the French and the Poles, they were unable to participate in the eventual liberation of their country. During the Allied advance from the Seine to the German frontier, the Czech brigade was given the unglamorous job of masking off the German garrison which obstinately held out in Dunkirk until the German surrender in the West.

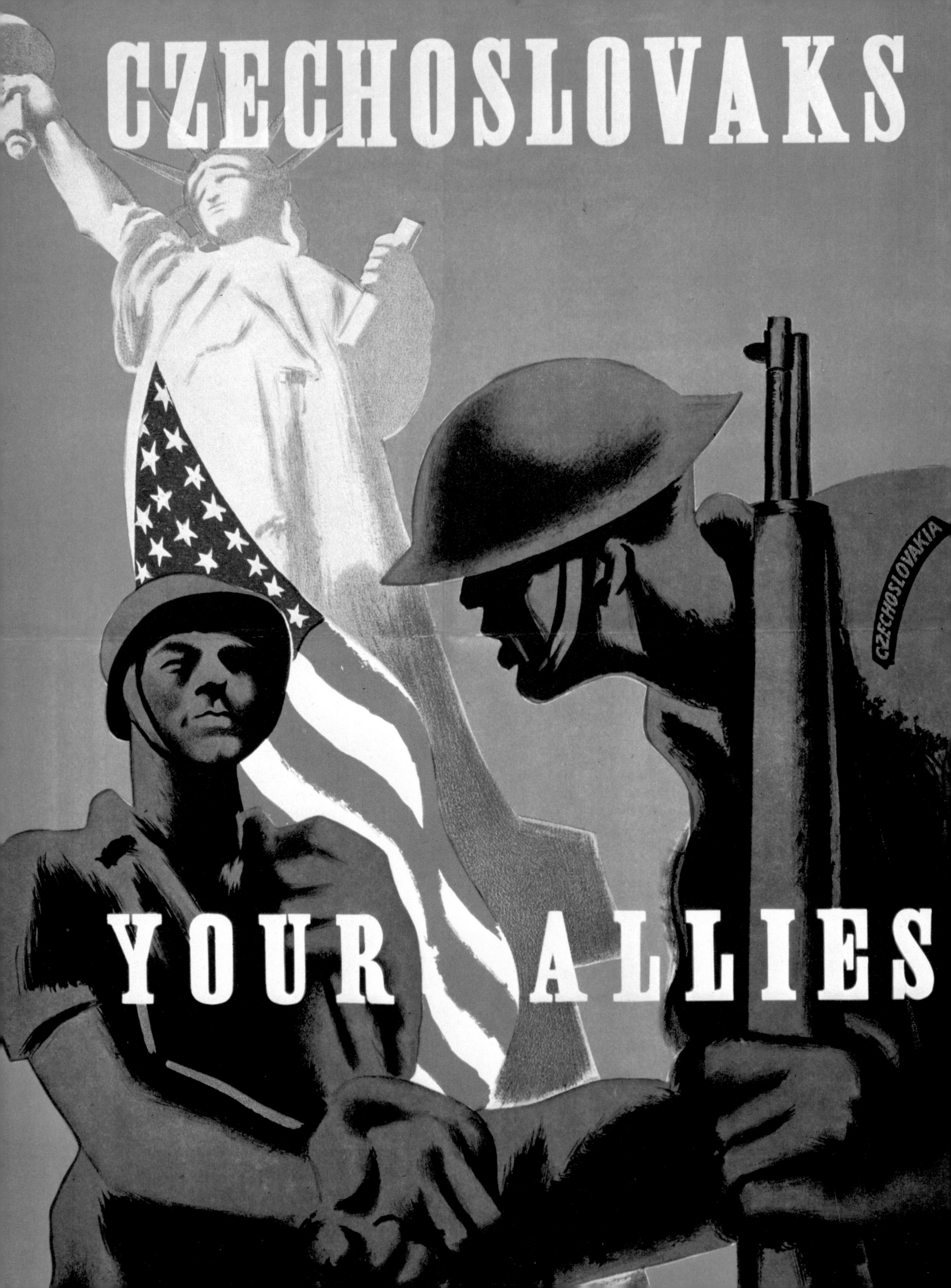
CZECHOSLOVAKS
CZECHOSLOVAKIA
YOUR ALLIES

Poland's overseas armies

Despite the total collapse of the Polish Army during the Blitzkrieg campaign of 1939 and the subsequent partition of the country by Germany and the Soviet Union, Poland had by no means been knocked out of the war. Her underground "Home Army" grew in strength and trained against the day when it could rise and fight the invaders; and abroad thousands of Polish soldiers, sailors, and airmen carried on the fight in foreign service.

To start with the only way in which they could do this was to escape to the West via Rumania, a long and hazardous route which some 100,000 Poles managed to cover. The Red Army, during its stab-in-the-back advance into eastern Poland, rounded up about 217,000 Polish prisoners of war. And the first chance that the free Poles had to hit back at the Germans came during the Norwegian campaign of 1940.

As a dramatic curtain-raiser, the Polish submarine *Orzel* torpedoed the German transport

General Władysław Sikorski was born in Poland in 1881. He served with distinction in the Polish Legion during World War I and the struggle against Bolshevism. In 1939 he went to Paris, to take command of a provisional Polish army. When Warsaw fell he became head of the Polish government-in-exile. In 1941, when Hitler attacked Russia, he made an alliance with Stalin, with the intention of forming a new Polish army from the P.O.W.s taken by Russia during the invasion of Poland. Thus his attention was drawn to the disappearance of several thousand Polish officers, who were later found in mass graves near Katyn. He was killed in an air crash in July 1943.

1. *Alert! A stand-to-Arms by Polish troops serving with the Red Army.*
2. *The face of confidence: Polish troops embus for the front in a Red Army truck.*

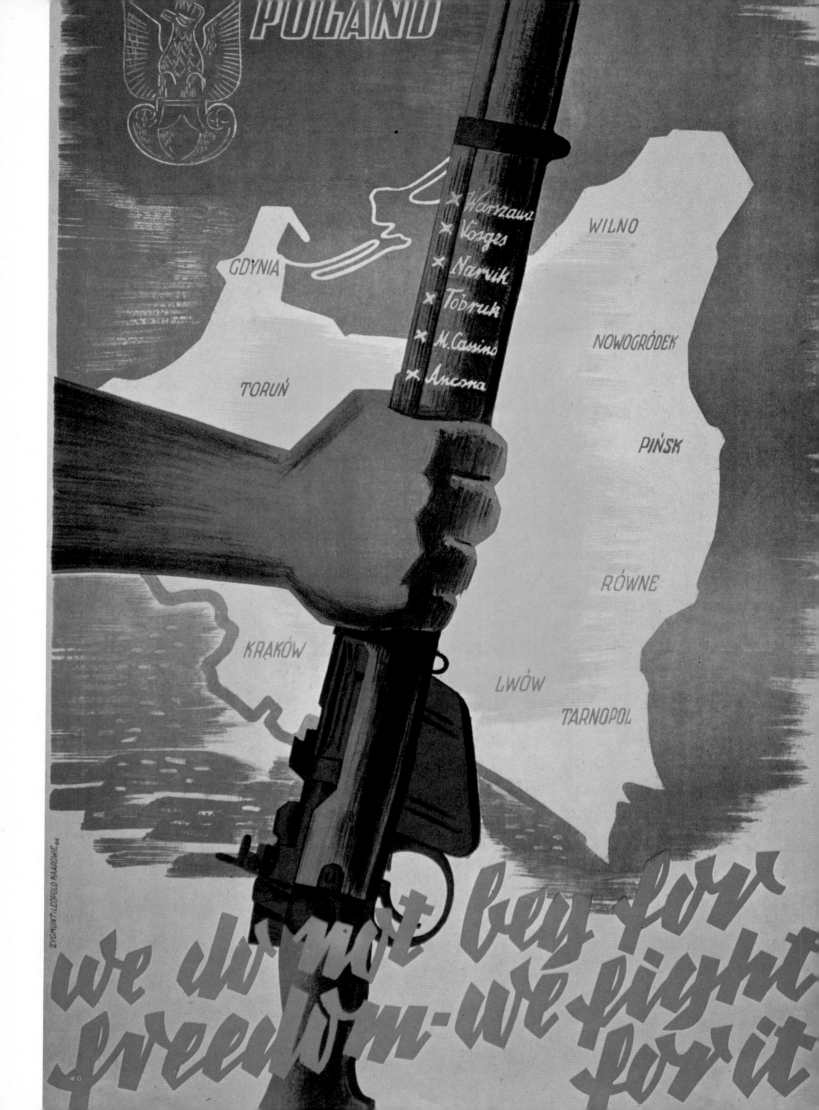

3. *A reminder of why Europe went to war in 1939: Poland's determination to fight for her freedom.*
4. *Polish troops in Tobruk. They took over from the Australians who denied Rommel the fortress in the spring of 1941, and held it until the 8th Army raised the siege in Operation "Crusader".*
5. *Polish regiment heads out to battle in the Western Desert.*
6. *Men of the Polish Carpathian Cavalry Brigade which rode from Syria to join the British after the fall of France in 1940.*

o de Janeiro, heading for orway packed with German oops, in the morning of April 8. his incident should have been strumental in bringing Norway a full alert and preventing e German Navy from achieving rprise when it struck at arvik, Trondheim, and Bergen e following morning. This did t happen; the Germans secured eir foothold, and the Allies astily prepared an expeditionary rce to send to Norway. The suing fiasco was the first ne that British and German rces clashed in World War II— d it was also the first time at free Polish forces saw action. his happened at Narvik, here General Béthouart's 1st *hasseur* Light Division landed tween April 28 and May 7. included the 1st Carpathian *hasseur* Demi-Brigade under eneral Bohusz-Szysko, which ayed a key rôle in the capture Narvik – an empty victory, lowed almost immediately by e evacuation of the Allied rce and its return to Britain. During the Polish campaign the olish air force put up a heroic d punishing fight against the

Luftwaffe before being removed from the board, and many pilots and aircrew managed to escape to the West. There, re-trained for action in modern fighters, their first big chance for action came with the Battle of Britain. The Polish fighter pilots could not be faulted as far as fighting spirit was concerned, but their discipline in the air often wavered. The R.A.F. ace, Stanford Tuck, found himself obliged to ground Polish pilots for "tearing off on a private war" instead of maintaining formation; but later in the Battle Tuck was touched and honoured when his Polish pilots solemnly presented him with a set of Polish Air Force "wings" to wear on his tunic.

The next theatre in which the free Poles played a prominent rôle was in North Africa. After the Australians under General Morshead had thwarted Rommel's dash on Tobruk and beaten off all his early attacks, they were relieved by General Scobie's 70th Division. This unit, which held Tobruk until the siege was raised by Auchinleck's "Crusader" offensive in November/ December 1941, contained

5

6

7

8

7-9. *Polish pilots of No. 303 Squadron, R.A.F., based at Northolt. Many a R.A.F. fighter commander was forced to take firm action against the fierce, freelance tactics of Polish fighter pilots under his command.*
10. *Formation flying by the fighting Poles: No. 303 Squadron in echelon.*

9

General Kopanski's Polish brigade. The Poles in Tobruk threw themselves into the task of strengthening the perimeter defences and rapidly established a reputation for aggressive dash and *panache*. One Polish battalion commander got into the habit of strolling across No Man's Land to the Italian line and haranguing its troops in good Italian on their stupidity in remaining allies of the Germans; and this went on until one evening he was greeted with "Three cheers for the Poles!"

But there was nothing light-hearted about the Polish attitude to the war. They were grim and tough fighters and even the men of Rommel's *Afrika Korps* did not relish the thought of falling into their hands. British Intelligence officers interrogating German prisoners found it very useful to have Polish sentries standing by during the questioning. Even recalcitrant prisoners tended to modify their attitude on a hint that co-operation would result in their being placed in British, rather than Polish, custody.

By this time the war had been transformed by the German invasion of the Soviet Union. This not only brought Russia into the war, but radically changed the status of the Polish prisoners of war taken in September 1939 and imprisoned in Russia. Recruiting of Polish volunteers was intensified, first as an emergency measure during the first two years of German victories in Russia, and later for political reasons. In formulating his long-term plans for Poland, Stalin did not ignore the value of establishing a Polish "army in exile", under the aegis of the Red Army, as well as a government in exile formed of sound Communists.

For 4,143 Polish officers, this new move came much too late. These were the men exhumed at Katyn, all of the men captured in 1939 and taken to Russia. The Katyn controversy has been covered elsewhere (see Chapter 103), but the investigations carried out on the site proved conclusively that the bodies were those of the men imprisoned in a Soviet camp at Kozelsk. When the other P.O.W.s were released on the German invasion of Russia (in many cases after months of mistreatment in Soviet hands), urgent enquiries were made as to the whereabouts of their missing comrades—enquiries which met with stubborn silence from Moscow. During these enquiries,

11. *General Sikorski takes the salute at a march-past by Polish troops in Scotland.*

12. *Swearing in new recruits. Polish volunteers from South America lay their hands on a tank and swear the oath of allegiance as they join an armoured regiment in England.*

11

12

13. *Poles fight with the "Overlord" host: a tank commander gives his orders during the advance from the Seine.*
14. *Polish troops with their wounded at Monte Cassino. When the abbey finally fell, it was the Polish flag that was hoisted over the ruins.*

eutenant-Colonel Berling of the ⅰlish General Staff was shocked ⸱ a remark from M. Merkulov, ⸱e deputy head of the Soviet ⸱cret Police. When Berling men⸱ned the men in the Kozelsk ⸱mp, Merkulov said "No, not ⸱ose. We made a great mistake ⸱th them."

One of the Polish officers who ⸱as allowed to go to the West was ⸱eneral Anders. He had been ⸱ven the job of mustering the ⸱cleus of the new Polish Army ⸱ the training camps of Tets⸱ye and Tatishchevo. Anders ⸱thered some 46,000 ex-P.O.W.s ⸱d it was at this time that the ⸱tremely small percentage of ⸱ficers began to sow seeds of ⸱ubt in his mind. After much ⸱essure, Stalin agreed to transfer ⸱o or three Polish divisions to ⸱rsia, where a new Polish corps ⸱s to be raised.

This was the origin of the ⸱lish II Corps, to which the ⸱itish contributed the Polish ⸱arvik veterans and Kopanski's ⸱igade. The II Corps consisted of the 3rd Carpathian Division, the 5th Kresowa Division, and the 2nd Armoured Brigade. It was earmarked for service in Italy under the command of 8th Army; General Anders was to lead it, and the unit landed in Italy in February 1944.

So it was that Anders and the Polish II Corps were given a real baptism of fire: the struggle for Cassino. Its troops attacked with superb dash but suffered murderous losses and Anders was forced to call them off. Before it finally battled its way on to the ruined crest of Monte Cassino, the II Corps lost 3,779 men. It was a heavy price to pay for the glory of being hailed as the "conquerors of Cassino", and for raising the Polish flag over the shattered monastery.

Further hard fighting still lay ahead for Anders and II Corps in Italy during 1944 and the spring of 1945; but in September 1944 came the chance for the Polish troops recruited in Russia. This was the Polish 1st Army, serving under Marshal Rokossovsky's army group. The great Soviet summer offensive carried the Red Army to the gates of Warsaw before it petered out; but the Polish Home Army had already launched its attempt to seize Warsaw. While the Germans ringed off the Poles in Warsaw, the Red Army lay immobile on the eastern bank of the Vistula. Desperate attacks across the Vistula by the Polish 1st Army managed to establish bridgeheads in Warsaw itself and establish tenuous contact with the insurgents, but nothing could be done to prevent their gradual destruction. Apart from the tragedy of the Rising itself, the Poles of the 1st Army were in an agonising position: the official Soviet attitude was that the Rising was the act of "dangerous criminals".

So it was that both in the West and the East, Polish troops fought with honour for Allied victory and their country's freedom.

Volunteers from Holland

Holland was the first of the Western neutral powers to fall under the hammer of the German offensive in May 1940. Five days were sufficient to overrun the country and force the Dutch Army to capitulate–but the Dutch nation was by no means knocked out of the war. The Queen and her government emigrated to England and the Netherlands officially remained in the war, with the resources of the Dutch overseas empire, navy, and mercantile marine at the service of the Allied cause.

The first Dutch troops who refused to accept surrender began to arrive in England on May 15. They had had wildly different adventures. One artillery unit fought its way south through the German lines, crossed Belgium and northern France, and ended up at Cherbourg, whence it was ordered to England by the Dutch government. One Dutch soldier decided quite simply to "go it alone" and set off on foot, lying up by day and marching by night. At one time

he was fired on as a deserter, but he kept walking–across Belgium, across France, over the Pyrenees, and across Spain, ending up at Lisbon, from where he was conveyed to England to join up in the Free Dutch brigade. A steady trickle of escapees managed to cross the Channel in following months. Typical of them were a party of Dutch P.O.W.s who had been fishing off the Dutch coast under armed guards. A sudden mutiny put the Germans over the side and the Dutch P.O.W.s set off for England, where they duly arrived–this incident took place as late as 1942.

The Dutch Legion formed in Britain retained the original Dutch Army uniform until July 1940, when its soldiers were re-equipped with standard British battle-dress. They sported the Dutch lion on the left shoulder with the title "Nederland" below. On June 21 the Dutch government-in-exile called up all Dutch male nationals resident in the United Kingdom, which considerably swelled the numbers of

the Dutch Legion. In July the Legion was given its first operational duties; coastal and airfield defence. A British Military Mission to the Dutch Forces was established on August 12, 1940; and the "Royal Netherlands Brigade 'Princess Irene'" was a going concern by the end of the year.

There had been no Dutch air force as such, the air service being divided into Army and Naval Air Services. Luftwaffe strafing eliminated most of the land-based aircraft but many aircrew of the Naval Air Service managed to escape to England in their Fokker seaplanes. Once in England they were incorporated into the R.A.F., flying Coastal Command patrols; and Ansons with R.A.F. markings and the distinctive Dutch yellow triangle became a familiar and welcome sight on Britain's coastal approaches.

When Japan struck in December 1941 the Royal Dutch Navy in the Far East had a decisive rôle to play. The Dutch Navy had a

fighting tradition second to none. It had been beaten only once in its long history: at Camperdown in 1797. Now it formed an integral part of the hastily-formed Allied naval squadron given the task of defending the Dutch East Indies, "A.B.D.A.", the initials standing for American-British-Dutch-Australian. It never had anything like a fair chance, with the Japanese dominating the skies and keeping touch with every move the Allies made. But under the command of Rear-Admiral Karel Doorman, flying his flag in the Dutch cruiser *De Ruyter*, the A.B.D.A. force made valiant efforts to disrupt the development of the Japanese advance. Doorman's polyglot cruiser-destroyer force was strong enough on paper but it never had the chance to settle down and learn to operate as an integrated unit. Whittled down by torpedo attacks and repeated gunnery engagements, Doorman's squadron gallantly went to its doom in the Battle of the Java sea, its duty done in vain.

1. *To fight again. Two Dutch officers arrive in England after crossing the North Sea in a sailing canoe.*
2. *The Christmas spirit, 1940. Free Dutch soldiers at their Christmas dinner in England.*
3. *The Free Dutch versus the Home Guard. In this "invasion" of Birkenhead in August 1941, the Free Dutch swept the Home Guard defenders out of the way and took the town regardless of "casualties".*
4. *Every inch a Tommy–Free Dutch troops drill in British kit.*

This is America...

...where men have left their peacetime jobs to defend the liberties that are their birthright, where the might of a free people is marching toward victory ★ This is your America

...Keep it Free!

The internees: ordeal of the civilians

Many factors made World War II a total war. There was the very *extent* of the conflict – from the Volga to the Channel, from the Sahara to the North Cape, from India to Hawaii, and from the Aleutian Islands to Australia. There was the tremendous impact of aerial bombardment. And there was the unholy partnership between modern technology and primeval hatreds which produced the Nazi genocide programme. All this was on an unprecedented scale and out of all proportion to anything seen in previous wars. But one aspect of World War II was not new. This was the fate of the age-old victims of any war: the civilians betrayed by the failure of politicians in peacetime and caught up by the clash of armies in war.

Until World War I the fate of civilians in war had not varied much. There was conscription and rising prices and falling amounts of food and other supplies. Civilians in occupied territory would get plundered by the armies of both sides whenever they marched through, and made to suffer for the work of compatriot resistance groups. But in general the civilians remained essentially localised in the countries of their birth until the floodgates of emigration were lifted in the 19th Century – and the first major sifting of the population of the world began.

There were German and Russian Jews in Britain and France, and British and French governesses in Germany and Russia. The United States, with a ravenous labour market, took in practically every nationality in Europe like a parched sponge. But at the same time the new emergent nations were creating a fierce new awareness of national patriotism which was poles apart from this new intermingling. As the 20th Century began, and international tension built up towards the explosion of 1914, the "foreigner within the gate" took on a new and more ominous significance. And during World War I the inevitable results occurred. Deliberately-inspired hate campaigns ended up with completely innocent foreigners being beaten up and having their shop windows smashed by loyalist mobs.

The Armistice of 1918 did not lay the ghost of nationalist hatred. Far from it. The story of the territorial grievances outstanding from the end of World War I have already been told, together with the grim events in the 1920s and 1930s, from the French occupation of the Ruhr to the end of the Spanish Civil War. Germany, spared from war by Anglo-French inertia, buckled down to the task of expelling or incarcerating her Jewish population. Millions died in Russia during Stalin's purges. In the Far East the

1. A promise not always kept. Thousands of loyal Americans were rounded up and interned on account of their original nationality.
2. Japanese fishermen and cotton planters put behind bars as soon as the news of Pearl Harbor came in.

2

1841

decades-old Sino-Japanese conflict broke out again and the martyrdom of the Chinese people began. By the outbreak of the European conflict in September 1939 the nationalist tensions of 1914 had been not only intensified but enlarged onto a far wider canvas.

To start with the tempo of civilian internment was slow. The tensions of August 1939 had been obvious to all and the number of German, French,

3. The phobia of "the enemy within."
4. Japanese aliens in California.
5. and 6. Internment camp for aliens at Fort Meade, Maryland – complete with watch-towers and sentinels.

LOOK WHO'S Listening

THIS POSTER IS PUBLISHED BY THE HOUSE OF SEAGRAM AS PART OF ITS CONTRIBUTION TO THE NATIONAL VICTORY EFFORT

IN THE GRIP OF
JAPANESE
CO-PROSPERITY

7 and British civilians caught on what had suddenly become enemy territory was vestigial. Formalities were duly observed and diplomats handed their passports. Defeated Poland was the first to suffer: not merely the Jews, who had long been marked down for elimination, but the "intelligentsia" of the country—prominent civilians, writers, artists, and politicians, who had at all costs to be prevented from keeping alive Poland's will to

7-10. *The other side of the coin: American and British internees in Japanese hands.*
8. *Early days. A holiday look prevails in the Santo Tomas camp, Manila, in the Philippines.*
9. *Japanese soldiers pause at a stall in the Santo Tomas camp.*
10. *Primitive huts in Santo Tomas.*

resist.

The first big change came with the runaway German victories of May-June 1940 which ended up with the French armistice and the German occupation of the Channel Islands. For the first time appreciable numbers of British civilians were rounded up in the conquered countries and shipped off to internment camps in Germany. Here their treatment was austere but conducted according to the Geneva Convention – after initial hardships in "sorting" camps in Belgium and France before the deportations began. The lot of the Channel Islanders was harder. They were an occupied part of the United Kingdom. They were forced to submit to repeated drafts of manpower for labour in Germany, and by 1944-45 the problem of food supplies was rapidly approaching starvation level. Total disaster was only averted by Red Cross intervention and the end of the war in Europe.

Italy's entry into the war in June 1940 saw the first large-internment of civilians in Britain. The problem of housing them was solved mainly by shipping them off to Canada, running the threat of U-boat attacks, but with spacious camps and fair treatment at the far end of the route.

Across the Atlantic the problem of what to do with enemy civilians did not arise until December 1941 – but there the targets were far more defined. For a start there was the American German *Bund*, a well-knit Nazi network with official headquarters and public rallies hailing the Führer's latest victories and pledging support to him. The Italian population of the United States was far higher than in Britain – but it had put down deep roots. The Duce's new Empire was far away and there was a general tendency for Italians in the United States to consider themselves American citizens – epitomised by the Order of the Sons of Italy in America which solemnly pledged allegiance to the Stars and Stripes.

When America was plunged into war by Pearl Harbor the situation, as far as Germans and Italians were concerned, was therefore comparatively straightforward *Bund* members and leaders were rounded up and headquarters closed down, and the crews of Italian ships in American ports duly interned.

Matters were far more complicated – and heartbreaking – for the Japanese in America. They were branded as the villains of the piece for the shock of Pearl

11. *Aliens register in Britain.*
12. *On the way to internment.*
13. *A solemn profession of loyalty: the Supreme Council of the Order of the Sons of Italy in America pledge their allegiance to the United States in front of the Liberty Bell.*

14. *A tagged collection of guns, cameras, and radios surrendered by aliens in New York City.*
15. *Allegiance to the other side. German-Americans give the Nazi salute at the German Day Rally, October 4, 1940, in Madison Square Garden.*
16. *Federal officers point to the huge swastika on the ceiling of the American Bund Camp at Andover, New Jersey.*

Harbor. Official whitewash for the attack hinted at widespread "fifth-column" activity, not only on Oahu but in the homeland itself. Familiar scenes of nationalist hostility took place in America as mass Japanese internement began. It was an agonising and uphill fight for the second-generation Japanese-Americans to gain recognition. When they did they won renown in no uncertain manner — particularly the Japanese-American "Mo' Bettah" battalion in the bloody attacks across the Rapido river during the Battle of Cassino.

The big internment camps set up by the Americans were clean, well-ordered, and humane-but across the Pacific the scene was totally different. Immediately

after the sweeping Japanese victories in South-East Asia and the Pacific there was a definite distinction drawn between military and civilian prisoners. To the Japanese a surrendered soldier was disgraceful, human filth, a betrayer of his country, to whom no Western concept of humanity or justice should apply. But to start with the civilians were deluged with clumsy propaganda blandishments of the brave new world awaiting them in Japan's "Co-Prosperity Sphere". It did not take long for the Japanese to realise that European civilians in their charge were not reacting according to plan; and the ordeal of the civilians began.

It is a story best kept short—of the civilian prisoners given rations hopelessly inadequate for Western metabolisms and doomed to slow starvation, forbidden to resort to barter to supplement their scanty food supplies. In the main internment camps on Sumatra and Java—Tjideng and Kramat, Struisweg and Brastagi—conditions rapidly slumped to create all the horrors discovered by the Allies in concentration camps such as Belsen, Buchenwald, and Ravensbrück, with all the hideous refinements of tropical diseases thrown in. Hunger-strikes, demonstrations, and break-out attempts were put down with the utmost cruelty by the sadists of the *Kempetai*—Imperial Japan's Gestapo.

Thus the ordeal of the civilians was one of the oldest aspects of war, brought up to date and refined by the processes of 20th Century war. The ultimate victims of the conflict, they could not escape the sufferings—both mental and physical—of the fighting men.

17

18

17. *When all seemed set fair for Italian victory: Italian seamen cheerfully give the Fascist salute aboard the liner* Conte Biancamano *as they are interned at Brooklyn.*
18. *Whiling away the months of captivity: Italian seamen, interned at Fort Missoula, Montana, make ship models.*

19

Starve him with Silence

WAR Secrets

706

THIS POSTER IS PUBLISHED BY THE HOUSE OF SEAGRAM AS PART
OF ITS CONTRIBUTION TO THE NATIONAL VICTORY EFFORT

20

BEWARE

TROOP TRAIN WRECKED
BLAME CARELESS TALK

THE WALLS HAVE EARS

Joe Leonard

19. and 20. *Expressive of the
basic fear behind all the
internments – one of the
greatest propaganda
achievements of World War II,
the "Fifth Column".*
21. *Long banks of typists record
the particulars of registering
aliens.*

21

Previous page: *U.S. armour heads for Coutances past a knocked-out Panther tank.*
△ △ *American personnel carriers await the order to move up.*
△ *General Courtney H. Hodges, Bradley's able successor as head of the American 1st Army.*

It is now time to return to the Western Front, where on July 25 General Bradley began Operation "Cobra".

On that day Army Group "B", under Field-Marshal von Kluge, who was now also C.-in-C. West, consisted of:

1. from the coastal battery at Merville to the area of Caumont-l'Eventé: 5th *Panzerarmee* (General Eberbach) comprising LXXXVI Corps, I and II *Waffen*-S.S. Panzer Corps, LXXIV Corps, with between them 11 divisions, including two Panzer and two *Panzergrenadier* (about 645 tanks); and

2. from Caumont-l'Eventé to the western coast of the Cotentin peninsula: 7th Army (General Hausser) astride the Vire with three corps of 13 divisions: on the right bank of the river XLVII Panzer Corps and II Parachute Corps with between them six infantry divisions and on the left bank LXXXIV Corps with one *Panzergrenadier* and two Panzer divisions (about 190 tanks).

But, we would repeat, there are divisions and divisions. Let us take the case of LXXXIV Corps, which was going to bear the brunt of the attack. Its 91st, 243rd, and

352nd Divisions had only 2,500 rifles between them, after the fierce fighting in the *bocage,* and its three armoured divisions (*"Lehr"* and 2nd S.S. *"Das Reich"* Panzer, and 17th *"Götz von Berlichingen" Panzergrenadier*) were down to something like half their establishment. It is over 21 miles as the crow flies from the Vire at Saint Lô to the bay of Lessay, but the front, with its many twists and turns, was much longer and the German 7th Army could not be expected to hold it. Bradley brought up no less than 12 divisions, including four armoured:

1. on the left the American VII Corps (Major-General J. L. Collins), with its left flank along the Vire, was given the job of making the breakthrough. The 30th, 4th, and 9th Divisions were engaged in first echelon along a four mile front. The breach came in the Marigny area and the 1st Infantry and the 2nd and 3rd Armoured Divisions poured through south and south-west, not, however, going beyond Coutances on their right, so as to leave the way open for VIII Corps; and

2. VIII Corps (Major-General T. H.

Middleton) had the 8th, 79th, 83rd, and 90th Infantry and the 4th and 6th Armoured Divisions and, by a frontal attack, seized Coutances and pressed on to Avranches. When it reached Pontaubault on the Brittany border, it was to come under General George S. Patton's 3rd Army, which was to exploit this success towards the Loire and the Seine.

The 1st Army attacks

The attack of July 25 had the benefit of exceptionally powerful air preparation, the details of which were drawn up by General Bradley and Air Chief-Marshal Leigh-Mallory. On July 24 4,000 tons of bombs fell on LXXXIV Corps' positions. During the morning of the following day no fewer than 1,880 four-engined and twin-engined bombers, and 550 fighter-bombers dropped 4,150 tons of bombs opposite the American VII Corps front to a depth of a mile and a half and on the bridges upstream of the Vire from Saint Lô. By special orders from Bradley, who

did not want the terrain to be pitted with deep craters, only light bombs and napalm were used.

In spite of all precautions, the bombing caused casualties to the tune of 111 dead and 490 wounded in VII Corps. Amongst the dead was Lieutenant-General McNair, C.-in-C. of the "shadow" army group ostensibly stationed in south-east England to deceive the enemy into expecting a landing across the Straits of Dover. These were tragic losses: on the enemy side the bombing cut a swathe of death through the defences. "Nothing could withstand it," wrote the German historian Paul Carell. "Trenches, gun-emplacements: ploughed up. Petrol-, ammunition- and supply-dumps: set on fire." The Panzer-"*Lehr*" Division, in particular, down to 5,000 men, was heavily knocked about: "at least half its personnel was put out of action: killed, wounded, buried alive or driven out of their minds. All the tanks and guns in the forward positions were wiped out. Every road in the area was made useless."

Neither Colonel-General Hausser nor Field-Marshal von Kluge expected an attack of such violence from the Ameri-

△ ◁ *American armour crashes forward along the road and through fields in the lightning advance after the breakthrough at Saint Lô.*
△ *Technician 5th Grade Floyd L. Meyer of Potter Valley, California, examines the aftermath of a strafing run by Allied fighter-bombers: a knocked-out SdKfz 4/1 Opel Type S/SSM "Maultier" (Mule) carrier fitted with a ten-tube 15-cm* Panzerwerfer 42. *Note the dead crewman in the foreground.*

The American M3 armoured personnel carrier

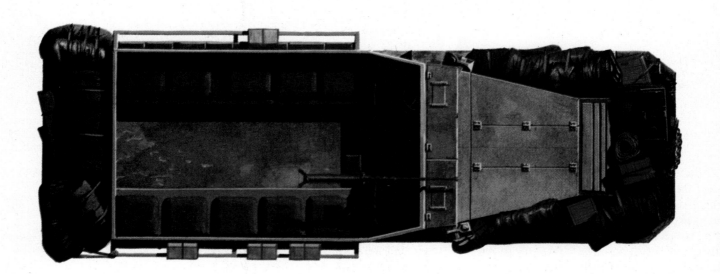

Weight: 10 tons.
Crew: 13.
Armament: one .5-inch Browning M2 machine gun.
Armour: hull front 13-mm, sides and rear 6-mm.
Engine: one White 160 AX inline, 147-hp.
Speed: 47 mph on roads, 35 mph cross-country.
Range: 220 miles on roads.
Length: 20 feet 9⅝ inches.
Width: 7 feet 3½ inches.
Height: 7 feet 5 inches.

an 1st Army between the Vire and the Channel. General von Choltitz, commanding LXXXIV Corps, who had seen it coming and whose warning had not been heeded by his superiors, now had to rely on his own resources to plug the gap created by the annihilation of the Panzer-"Lehr" Division. On July 26 Collins was able to pass his 2nd and 3rd Armoured Divisions (respectively Major Generals Edward H. Brooks and Leroy H. Watson) through his infantry lines. By evening the 3rd had passed through Marigny and was on its way to Coutances and the 2nd was patrolling through Saint Gilles and Canisy, some seven to eight miles from its point of departure.

The 2nd and 116th Panzer Divisions were hastily withdrawn from the 5th *Panzerarmee* in the Caen area but did not get to the breach until July 29, by which time it was widening every hour. There was therefore no alternative for LXXXIV Corps but to retreat, and do so quickly, as its left flank had been pierced in the area of Périers by the American VIII

Corps. The direction this retreat was to take gave rise to a conflict between the LXXXIV Corps and 7th Army commanders. The latter, anxious to retain some coherence in his dispositions, wanted Choltitz to withdraw south-eastwards, whereupon the latter protested vehemently that if he were to do this he would be opening the way for the enemy to get into Brittany. This is what happened, in fact; Kluge wrongly attributed the blame to Choltitz and replaced him by Lieutenant-General Elfeldt. Choltitz had no difficulty in clearing himself and was rewarded with the command of *Gross Paris*.

Coutances and Avranches captured

On July 28 the U.S. 4th Armoured Division (Major-General John S. Wood) took Coutances and that same night got across

Major-General Joseph "Lightning Joe" Collins was born in 1896 and graduated from West Point Military Academy in 1917. He was a battalion commander of the 18th Infantry Regiment in Koblenz after World War I. Between the wars he served both as an infantry and artillery instructor. In 1941 Collins was chief-of-staff of VII Corps and then of the Hawaii Department. Early in 1943 he commanded the 25th Division in the last stages of the campaign that drove the Japanese off the island of Guadalcanal. Collins was then transferred to Europe to command VII Corps in the battle for Normandy. Here he captured Cherbourg 20 days after D-Day and then spear-headed the break-out at the western side of the Cotentin peninsula. Later his corps broke through the *Westwall*, took Cologne and Aix-la-Chapelle, closed the pincer round the Ruhr from the south, and then pushed on to meet the Russians at Dessau on the Elbe. He had an enviable reputation as a hard, yet flexible, infantry commander.

△ *U.S. infantry take advantage of a bursting white phosphorus grenade to rush across a street in Brest, preparatory to clearing a German-held house.*

the Sienne at Cérences. Twenty-four hours later 6th Armoured Division (Major-General Robert W. Grow), moving on the right flank of the 4th, crossed the See and took Avranches. Facing them there was absolute confusion: continually compelled to move their headquarters by the advancing Americans, the German leaders lost all contact with their men, units got mixed up together and many of them, overtaken by Allied tanks, became moving pockets. At 0100 hours

on July 31 Lieutenant-General Speide telephoned Kluge: "The left flank ha collapsed."

Kluge calls for reinforcements . . .

A few minutes later the C.-in-C. Wes was again called: this time by Genera

is in Avranches and possibly also in Villedieu . . . These key positions for future operations must be held at all costs . . . All available strength from Saint Malo has been brought up. Spare naval and air force units, absolutely necessary for decisive struggle which will determine future of bridgehead, . . . impossible to get. General Warlimont agrees to put matter before the Führer.

"C.-in-C. West describes the situation with impressive eloquence. It might even be asked if the enemy can in fact be stopped at this point. His air superiority is terrifying and stifles our every move. On the other hand all his movements are prepared and protected by air strength. Our losses of men and *matériel* are extraordinary. Morale of troops has suffered greatly from the enemy's constant withering fire, especially as all infantry units are now only hastily-assembled groups and can no longer offer solid and coordinated resistance. Behind the front lines the terrorists [resistance] feel the end is at hand and are becoming ever bolder. This, and the destruction of many communication installations, makes an ordered command very difficult."

Kluge therefore demanded reinforcements, and urgently, reminding O.K.W. of the example of the taxis of the Marne.

Faced with the development of Operation "Cobra", Hitler at O.K.W. finally gave up the obsession with a second landing north of the Somme which had dominated all his strategy since dawn on June 6.

. . . and gets them, but too late

Responding to Kluge's call for help, Hitler ordered Salmuth to withdraw LXXXI Corps and 85th and 89th Divisions from the 15th Army and send them at once to 5th *Panzerarmee*. Meanwhile Army Group "G", responsible for the defence of "Fortress Europe" between the Loire estuary and the Franco-Italian frontier, was ordered to send its LVIII Panzer Corps, 708th Infantry, and 9th Panzer Divisions to the 7th Army. The 9th Panzer was stationed in the Avignon area and the army group's commander, Colonel-General Blaskowitz, would have liked to see it replaced by the 11th Panzer, stationed in Montauban, as an Allied landing in Provence was expected.

General George S. Patton Jr. was born in 1885 and served with the American armoured forces in France during 1918. This experience led him to become a fanatical tank enthusiast, an interest he developed and expanded between the wars. In 1942 he was the commander of the American forces in the "Torch" landings, and at beginning of the next year he led U.S. II Corps for a short time. Patton headed the U.S. 7th Army during the invasion of Sicily, during which he led a wide sweeping movement to the west, capturing Palermo, and then drove through to Messina. Early in 1944 he was the commander of the "shadow" Allied army group in south-east England intended to deceive the Germans into thinking that a landing in the Pas-de-Calais was imminent. After the Normandy landings, Patton was given the command of the U.S. 3rd Army, which he led in its superb dash from the breakout at Avranches to Metz. The campaign was notable for Patton's almost total disregard of orders and of orthodox military methods. He raised the siege of Bastogne in the "Battle of the Bulge" and then continued his advance into Germany and Czechoslovakia. Patton, one of the most controversial generals of the last war, was without doubt one of the ablest "cavalry" generals ever. He died after an accident in Germany in 1945.

Farmbacher, commanding XXV Corps, to say that, responsible now for organising the defence of Brittany, he found that the Kriegsmarine and the Luftwaffe, sheltering respectively behind Dönitz and Göring, were being removed from his authority. At 1045 hours the wretched Field-Marshal got in touch with O.K.W. and gave General Warlimont, Chief of Operations, a realistic picture of the situation:

"C.-in-C. West . . . informs that enemy

The crew of an American M8 light armoured car pauses to watch a burning building in Canisy. Known to the British as the Greyhound, the M8 was armed with a 37-mm cannon and a .5-inch machine gun. Over 12,000 were built during the course of the war.

The Führer, as was to be expected, failed to see that this was common sense.

Patton's new objectives

Hitler's decisions, however, came too late, and it was like shutting the stable doors after the horses had bolted. On July 31 General Patton, who now had VIII Corps as well, learned from this corps H.Q. that the 4th Armoured Division had reached its objective at Sélune and that the bridge at Pontaubault was still in good order. He made up his mind at once: "All through military history", he cried, "wars have been lost because rivers weren't crossed." He sent off the 6th Armoured and 79th Infantry Divisions (Major-General Ira T. Wyche) towards Brest and the 4th Armoured and 8th Infantry (Major-General Donald Stroh) towards Rennes. The breach was complete, the German 7th Army was beaten

and LXXXIV Corps, from which most of the 20,000 prisoners taken by the Americans since July 25 had come, was virtually wiped out. On August 1 General Bradley, now commanding 21 divisions, including six armoured, took over the American 12th Army Group in accordance with decisions taken in London on the eve of "Overlord". He handed over his 1st Army to General Courtney H. Hodges, having no qualms about his successor:

"A quiet and methodical commander, he knew his profession well and was recognised in the army as one of our most able trainers of troops. Whereas Patton could seldom be bothered with details, Hodges studied his problems with infinite care and was thus better qualified to execute the more intricate operations. A steady, undramatic, and dependable man with great tenacity and persistence, Hodges became the almost anonymous inside man who smashed the German Seventh Army while Patton skirted the end."

The German *Panzerjäger* IV *"Nashorn"* (Rhinoceros)

Weight: 26.5 tons.
Crew: 5.
Armament: one 8.8-cm Pak 43/1 gun.
Armour: 51-mm front and 30-mm sides.
Engine: one Maybach HL 120 TRM, 300-hp.
Speed: 25 mph on roads, 16 mph cross-country.
Range: 133 miles on roads, 81 miles cross-country.
Length: 20 feet 4 inches.
Height: 9 feet 7$\frac{3}{4}$ inches.
Width: 9 feet 7$\frac{1}{4}$ inches.

A French resistance fighter poses in front of some of the evidence of the late German occupation of Rennes.

The 1st Army at this time included V, VII, and XIX Corps. It had transferred VIII Corps to the 3rd Army, fighting alongside it, and Bradley had also moved over to 3rd Army XII, XV, and XX Corps (respectively Major-Generals R. Cook, Wade H. Haislip, and Walton H. Walker). The new C.-in-C. 12th Army Group, promoted over the head of the impetuous Patton, six years his senior, did not much relish the idea of having to send him directives but acknowledged that "George" was a great-hearted and highly intelligent soldier who, in spite of his celebrated outbursts of temper, served him with "unbounded loyalty and eagerness".

The same occasion brought the formation of the British 21st Army Group, under General Montgomery, with the British 2nd Army, still under Sir Miles Dempsey, and the Canadian 1st Army (Lieutenant-General H. D. G. Crerar). On August 15, 21st Army Group was to have five corps of 16 divisions, including six armoured, and several brigades. This reorganisation of the land forces ought to have brought General Eisenhower to their head as previously agreed. Thinking that his presence was more necessary in England, he postponed taking over command until September 1. Montgomery therefore continued to send his directives to Bradley, whilst at the same time commanding his army group, hoping no doubt that he would get to Berlin before S.H.A.E.F. (Supreme Headquarters Allied Expeditionary Forces) came into being on the continent if Eisenhower's arrival were repeatedly postponed. This was to ignore American national feeling, not only at the front but also in the United States.

Hitler envisages withdrawal

In the afternoon of July 30 Colonel-General Jodl, having informed Hitler of his concern at the capture of Avranches, noted in his diary: "The Führer reacted favourably to the idea of an order for eventual withdrawal in France. This confirms that he thinks such an order is necessary at the present time.

"1615 hours: called Blumentritt (chief-of-staff to C.-in-C. West). Advised him in guarded terms to be ready for such an order, adding that certain actions had to be taken straight away within G.H.Q. and that he should put a small working party on to it from among the general staff."

The matter of withdrawal seemed virtually settled and Lieutenant-General Warlimont was designated as liaison officer with C.-in-C. West. But on the following morning, when the O.K.W. delegate was leaving, the Führer said: "Tell Field-Marshal von Kluge that his job is to look forwards to the enemy, not backwards!"

Warlimont was thus in an embarrassing situation, caught between the "yes" of July 30 and the "no" of the 31st. On August 3, the expected order from O.K.W. reached Kluge in the morning, but instead of confirming the withdrawal intimated by Jodl, it ordered a counter-attack. By driving towards Avranches Hitler hoped the 7th Army would trap those American forces which had ventured into Brittany. And, doing half Kluge's job for him, O.K.W. issued an order giving details for the operation. According to General Blumentritt:

"O.K.W. settled the precise divisions which were to be used and which were therefore to be taken out of the line as soon as possible. The exact limits of the sector in which the attack was to take place were laid down, as well as the routes to be taken and even the villages the troops were to pass through. These plans were all made in Berlin on large-scale maps and the opinions of the commanding generals in France were neither asked for nor encouraged."

The plan was to assemble an armoured mass on the left flank of the 7th Army under General von Funck, C.-in-C. XLVII Panzer Corps, attack towards Avranches through Mortain, and cut the communications of the American 3rd Army. But Hitler would not stop there. Funck was then to press on to Saint Lô and overwhelm the American 1st Army by an outflanking attack. This would give Germany an eleventh-hour game and match in the West.

More time needed

Kluge was dumbfounded when he read Hitler's directive. He wrote to Hitler on August 18, before he took poison, to say that, except for the one single division,

the 2nd Panzer, "the armoured units, after all the fighting they had done, were so weakened that they were incapable of any shock tactics . . . Your order was based on a completely erroneous supposition. When I first learned of it I immediately had the impression that I was being asked to do something which would go down in history as a grandiose and supremely daring operation but which, unfortunately, it was virtually impossible to carry out so that, logically, the blame would fall on the military commander responsible . . .

"On the basis of these facts I am still convinced that there was no possible chance of success. On the contrary: the attacks laid down for me could only make the situation of the Army Group decidedly worse. And that is what happened."

Kluge was in no position to claim freedom of action in face of this order, as stupid as it was absolute. He was aware that Hitler knew of the part he had played in the July 20 plot and that the slightest disobedience would cost him his life.

The discussion therefore centred less on the principles involved than on the date of the operation, which was to be called *"Lüttich"* (Liège). Hitler wanted to hold back until as many American divisions as possible had been drawn into the net; Kluge urged the threat to the left flank and even to the rear of the 7th Army and asked for a start on August 7, to which Hitler agreed.

Allied aircraft beat the Panzers

At dawn on D-day, helped by fog, XLVII Corps (116th and 2nd Panzer Divisions, 1st *"Leibstandarte"* and 2nd *"Das Reich"* S.S. Panzer Divisions) attacked between the See and the Sélune towards Avranches. Mortain fell fairly easily. But neither the American 30th Division (Major-General Leland S. Hobbs), though it had one battalion surrounded, nor the American VII Corps (Major-General J. L. Collins)

△ △ *The American advance under a smoke-blackened sky.*
△ *American troops round up a motley assortment of German prisoners-of-war.*

were thrown off their stride, and towards mid-day *"Das Reich"* was stopped less than two miles from Saint Hilaire-du-Harcouët, over 14 miles from its objective of Pontaubault.

The fog had lifted by now, and the Panzers were caught by hundreds of fighter-bombers, whose armour-piercing rockets again proved their deadly efficiency. The previous day General Bülowius thought he could guarantee the C.-in-C. 7th Army that 300 Luftwaffe fighters would be continuously sweeping the skies above the battlefield. These had been intercepted by Anglo-American fighters as soon as they took off from the Paris area.

Faced with this lack of success, Kluge gave it as his opinion that the German forces should hold on to what they had got, or even let go. The answer was an order to throw in II S.S. Panzer Corps (General Bittrich: 9th *"Hohenstaufen"* and 10th *"Frundsberg"* Panzer Divisions), to be withdrawn from the already depleted 5th *Panzerarmee*. Once more C.-in-C. West had to give in, in spite of vehement protests from General Eberbach, who was expecting a strong Anglo-Canadian attack southwards along the Caen–Falaise axis.

The Americans hesitate in Brittany

In spite of appearances, the first engagements of the American 3rd Army in Brittany betrayed a certain lack of initiative. This is not attributable in any way to lack of enthusiasm on Patton's part, but seems rather to have sprung from the inadequacy of his means of communication, which prevented his driving spirit from reaching down to his men. At the speed with which the armoured formations advanced, the supply of telephone cable within VIII Corps turned out to be insufficient, with a consequential overloading of the radio network and the use of squadrons of message-carrying jeeps to make up for it.

There were also interferences in the chain of command. The 4th Armoured Division received the order from VIII Corps, confirmed by General Bradley, not to go beyond Dinan until Saint Malo was cleared, whereas Patton had ordered it to drive on towards Brest (150

miles west of Rennes) with no intermediate objective. This left a gap in the enemy lines once Rennes had been passed, which 6th Armoured Division exploited along the axis Chartres–Paris, turning then towards Chateaubriant instead of Lorient. It was recalled to its original objective and found, when it got to Lorient, the German 265th Division in a defensive position around this large base. The 4th Armoured Division did manage to destroy the 266th Division, which had tried to take refuge inside Brest, but the German 2nd Parachute Division got there first and its commander, Lieutenant-General Ramcke, was not the sort of man to be impressed by cavalier raids, even ones made in considerable force, such as Patton's.

The responsibility for this Allied mix-up must belong to the Anglo-American high command, which had given two objectives to the forces breaking out of the Avranches bottleneck: the Breton ports and the rear areas of Army Group "B". This was how Eisenhower saw it when on August 5 he ordered only the minimum indispensable forces to be engaged in Brittany.

Patton sweeps on through the breach

This directive from Eisenhower gave Patton the chance to streak out through the enormous gap (65 miles) between Rennes and Nantes, which he did with XV Corps on the left, XX Corps in the centre, and XII Corps on the right with its right flank along the Loire. By August 7, XV Corps was in Laval and Château-Gontier whilst XII Corps liberated Nantes and Angers, ignoring enemy resistance in Saint Nazaire.

Thus Operation *"Lüttich"* did not deflect Montgomery and Bradley from their initial plan. On D-day the German XLVII Corps lost some 50 tanks out of the 120 with which it had started out at dawn. The American VII Corps, strengthened to five divisions, including one armoured, immediately went over to the counter-attack. This was the last chance for Army Group "B" to break out of the ring now beginning to take shape as Patton pushed ahead towards Le Mans. But Hitler obstinately refused to consider any withdrawal.

◀ *An American 57-mm anti-tank gun in action against a German bunker in the little Brittany port of Saint Malo.*
△ *Mixed British and American forces in the Caen area. While the American forces to the west were fanning out to the south, through Brittany, and also towards Paris, the British and Canadian troops in the Caen area were fighting a slow and remorseless battle on the northern edge of what was to become the "Falaise pocket".*

△ *Allied air power triumphs: a burnt-out German column in Normandy.*

Montgomery now had a chance to start a pincer movement which was to bring about the defeat of Army Group "B" between the Orne and the Dives on August 18 and the disgrace and suicide of the wretched Kluge. At 2330 hours on August 7 the Canadian 1st Army attacked south of Caen with its II Corps of four divisions, including two armoured. It was the beginning of Operation "Totalize", which was to capture Falaise.

At zero hour four mechanised columns, consisting of one armoured brigade on each flank and two motorised infantry brigades in the centre, crossed the first German line. When they had covered

CHAPTER 127
Slaughter at Falaise

etween two and three miles in the dark,
he Canadian and Scottish infantry,
rom the 2nd Canadian and 51st (High-
and) Divisions, left their vehicles to attack
he strongpoints of the German line,
luminated for them by green tracer
hells. At dawn it was clear that the H.Q.
f I S.S. Panzer Corps had been overrun,

the 89th Division, recently arrived on the
scene, had collapsed, and the 272nd looked
like giving way.

Once more the famous Panzer-Meyer
(Brigadier Kurt Meyer) and his 12th
"Hitlerjugend" Panzer Division saved
the situation with the help of 80 assault
guns and the 8.8-cm guns sent to them as

△ *British armoured cars on the
move in the Falaise area. Note
the ruins, the result of Allied
bombing.*

△ A British column pushes south from Caen. With the aid of the Americans, sweeping up north towards Argentan, Montgomery hoped to trap the 5th Panzerarmee at Falaise and wipe it out.

reinforcement. These young veterans, who had been in the line since June 8, were pitted against the Canadian 4th Armoured Division (Major-General G. Kitching) and the Polish 1st Armoured Division (Major-General S. Maczek), both of which were in action for the first time. The military cemeteries in the area bear witness to the valiant fighting of the Allied forces, but they did not succeed in breaking though and "Totalize" ground to a halt some ten miles short of Falaise on August 9.

General Leclerc's charge

On the same day the American XV Corps, having captured Le Mans, turned north. On its left the French 2nd Armoured Division (General Leclerc) was moving down to Alençon with the 79th Division in its wake. On the right the American 5th Armoured Division (Major-General

Lundsford E. Oliver) was on the road t Argentan, followed by the 90th Divisio which, newly commanded by Majo General Raymond S. MacLain, was t recover from the unfortunate reputatio it had acquired in the *bocage*. Consciou of the threat to his rear areas, Klug attempted to ward it off by improvising Panzergruppe "Eberbach" consisting c LXXXI Corps (General Kuntzen), 708tl Division (Lieutenant-General Wilck), an 9th Panzer Division (Lieutenant-Genera Jolasse) brought up from the south

The French 2nd Armoured Division vigorously led by General Leclerc, ra into the 9th Panzer Division on Augus 11, just as the Germans were movin, into their positions. As night fell th French took the bridges at Alenço whilst they were still intact. On thei right, the American 5th Armoured Divi sion had crossed the Sarthe and capture Sées, having overcome the feeble resis tance of the German 708th Division On the following day Leclerc had to figh

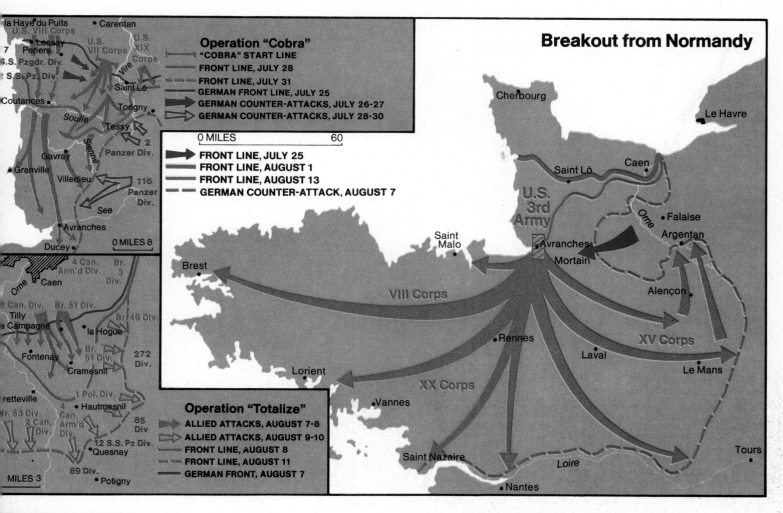

Breakout from Normandy

Operation "Cobra"
- "COBRA" START LINE
- FRONT LINE, JULY 28
- FRONT LINE, JULY 31
- GERMAN FRONT LINE, JULY 25
- GERMAN COUNTER-ATTACKS, JULY 26-27
- GERMAN COUNTER-ATTACKS, JULY 28-30

0 MILES   60

- FRONT LINE, JULY 25
- FRONT LINE, AUGUST 1
- FRONT LINE, AUGUST 13
- GERMAN COUNTER-ATTACK, AUGUST 7

Operation "Totalize"
- ALLIED ATTACKS, AUGUST 7-8
- ALLIED ATTACKS, AUGUST 9-10
- FRONT LINE, AUGUST 8
- FRONT LINE, AUGUST 11
- GERMAN FRONT, AUGUST 7

0 MILES 8

MILES 3

Labels on main map: Cherbourg, Le Havre, Caen, Saint Lô, Falaise, Argentan, Ome, U.S. 3rd Army, Saint Malo, Avranches, Mortain, Alençon, Brest, VIII Corps, Rennes, Laval, XV Corps, Le Mans, Lorient, XX Corps, Vannes, Saint Nazaire, Loire, Nantes, Tours

Labels on upper-left inset: la Haye du Puits, U.S. VIII Corps, Carentan, Lessay, Periers, U.S. VII Corps, U.S. XIX Corps, S.S. Pzgdr. Div., S.S. Pz. Div., Vire, Saint Lô, Coutances, Torigny, Soulle, Tessy, 2 Panzer Div., Sienne, Gavray, Granville, Villedieu, 116 Panzer Div., See, Avranches, Ducey

Labels on lower-left inset: 4 Can. Arm'd Div., Br. 3 Div., Ome, Caen, Can. Div., Br. 51 Div., Tilly, la Campagne, Br. 49 Div., la Hogue, Fontenay, Br. 51 Div., Cramesnil, 272 Div., retteville, 1 Pol. Div., Hautmesnil, Br. 53 Div., 4 Can. Arm'd Div., 85 Div., 2 Can. Div., 12 S.S. Pz Div., Quesnay, 89 Div., Potigny

△ *The Allied breakout from Normandy and the beginning of the Falaise pocket.*
◁ *British infantry prepare for an assault near Cagny.*

1865

it out with the 2nd *"Das Reich"* S.S. Panzer Division's forward units and the 116th Panzer Division, both of which Kluge had thrown into XV Corps' sector without any further regard for O.K.W.'s orders. The French nevertheless pushed their left flank as far as Carrouges and their right to the outskirts of Argentan.

At dawn on August 13 the American XV Corps was within 16 miles of Falaise, whilst the German 7th Army, caught up in the Condé-sur-Noireau–Tinchebray–Domfront area, had between 34 and 37 miles to go under enemy-controlled skies before it broke out of the pocket. In the afternoon, however, Haislip was ordered by Patton to stop and even to pull back the units "in the neighbourhood of Falaise or north of Argentan".

Why Bradley, via Patton, should have forbidden XV Corps to close the ring round Army Group "B" in the Falaise area has often been discussed, and the reasons given by the two generals in their memoirs do not carry conviction. No more do the arguments of General Eisen-

hower, who takes up Bradley's argument in his *Crusade in Europe,* saying:

"Mix-ups on the front occurred, and there was no way to halt them except by stopping troops in place, even at the cost of allowing some Germans to escape. In the aggregate considerable numbers of Germans succeeded in getting away. Their escape, however, meant an almost complete abandonment of their heavy equipment and was accomplished only by terrific sacrifices.

"I was in Bradley's headquarters when messages began to arrive from commanders of the advancing American columns, complaining that the limits placed upon them by their orders were allowing Germans to escape. I completely supported Bradley in his decision that it was necessary to obey the orders, prescribing the boundary between the army groups, exactly as written; otherwise a calamitous battle between friends could have resulted."

Certainly by exploiting his success on August 12 north of Argentan Haislip had

△ *A Sherman tank stands guard at the cross-roads in St. Martin-des-Besares as a carrier, towing a 57-mm anti-tank gun, and infantry pass through the village.*

The German *Jagdpanzer* 38(t) *"Hetzer"* (Baiter)

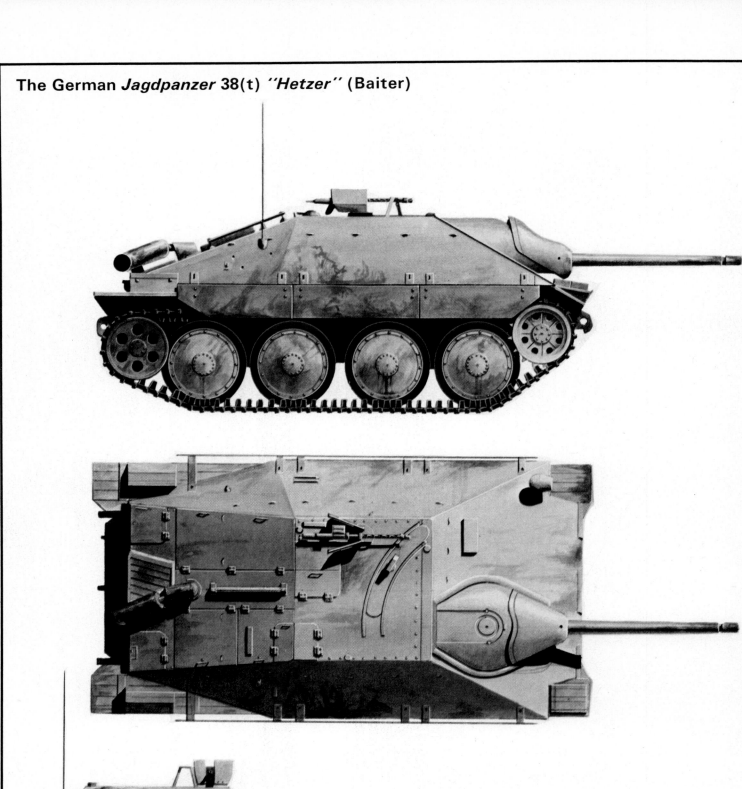

Weight: 17.6 tons.
Crew: 4.
Armament: one 7.5-cm PaK 39 L/48 gun with 41 rounds and one 7.92-mm MG 34 machine gun with 600 rounds.
Armour: front 60-mm, sides 20-mm, and rear 8-mm.
Engine: one EPA T2 inline, 158-hp.
Speed: 24 mph on roads, 10 mph cross-country.
Range: 111 miles on roads, 60 miles cross-country.
Length: 16 feet.
Height: 7 feet.
Width: 8 feet $4\frac{3}{4}$ inches.

overstepped the boundary between 12th and 21st Army Groups and risked running into the bombing destined for the Germans opposite the Canadian 1st Army. Was this boundary so vague, though, that the Anglo-American strategic air force, which was admittedly sometimes not very accurate, could not have been given clear orders? And the juncture between the Polish 1st Armoured Division and the American 90th did in fact take place without incident in the area of Chambois-sur-Dives on August 19.

This is why one is inclined to believe, like Jacques Mordal, that Eisenhower and Bradley, under the influence of Montgomery, were unwilling to content themselves with a "little" pincer around Falaise, as they were sure that they could bring about a much bigger one on the left bank of the Seine. They ignored the proverb of the bird in hand and when they said "stop" to Haislip they were intend-ing to give him a new and bigger task.

Kluge orders retreat

From August 15, Army Group "B" was on the retreat. Kluge did not wait for O.K.W. to confirm, but went ahead, setting in motion an operation involving two armies, seven corps, and no fewer than 23 divisions of all types. On August 17 General Dietrich, who had succeeded Eberbach as C.-in-C. 5th *Panzerarmee,* got I S.S. Panzer Corps out of the net and re-assembled the bits at Vimoutiers. But the Canadians took Falaise and the Polish 1st Armoured Division, advancing up the right bank of the Dives, established contact with the American V Corps (1st Army) which at that moment formed the southern arm of the pincer.

On August 20, according to Martin

△ *R.A.F. pilots burst from the "ready" tent after a call for fighter support from an R.A.F. Visual Control Point in the front line.*

Overleaf: *"Rocket-firing Typhoons at the Falaise Gap" by Frank Wootton. Against such massive Allied air superiority, the Germans lost almost all their matériel.*

△ *The British advance continues towards the east.*
△▷ *Happy soldiers of the French Forces of the Interior escort a German officer prisoner captured near Chartres.*

Blumenson, the author of the volume devoted to this episode in the official history of the U.S. Army, there occurred in 90th Division the "artillery-man's dream":

"Five battalions pulverized columns driving towards the Dives. American soldiers cheered when German horses, carts, trucks, volkswagens, tanks, vehicles, and weapons went flying into the air, disintegrating in flashes of fire and puffs of smoke."

Nevertheless I S.S. Panzer Corps, which had got out of this attack, collected together some 20,000 Germans from all units and, refusing to be dismayed, managed to find a crack in the Allied lines, through which they got 25 tanks and 60 guns. Included in these forces was General Hausser, C.-in-C. 7th Army, who was seriously wounded in the face. On the following day, however, all firing ceased in the Argentan–Nécy–Brieux–Chambois area. Here the Allies took 50,000 prisoners; there were 10,000 dead. The unhappy decision of August 13 thus left the Germans now with only 40,000 men. Fifteen divisions of Army Group "B" were wiped out in the course of this pitiless battle. According to Blumenson, one American officer, a veteran of the 1918 battles in the area of Soissons, Saint Mihiel, and the Argonne in 1918 and the

terrible bombing of London in 1940, said:

"None of these compared in the effect upon the imagination with what I saw yesterday south west of Trun . . . The grass and trees were vividly green as in all Normandy and a surprising number of houses (were) . . . untouched. That rather peaceful setting framed a picture of destruction so great that it cannot be described. It was as if an avenging angel had swept the area bent on destroying all things German.

"I stood on a lane, surrounded by 20 or 30 dead horses or parts of horses, most of them still hitched to their wagons and carts . . . As far as my eye could reach (about 200 yards) on every line of sight there were . . . vehicles, wagons, tanks, guns, prime movers, sedans, rolling kitchens, etc., in various stages of destruction.

"I stepped over hundreds of rifles in the mud and saw hundreds more stacked along sheds . . . I walked through a mile or more of lanes where the vehicles had been caught closely packed . . . I saw probably 300 field pieces and tanks, mounting large caliber guns, that were apparently undamaged.

"I saw no foxholes or any other type of shelter or field fortifications. The Germans were trying to run and had no place to run. They were probably too

The American Gun Motor Carriage M18 "Hellcat"

Weight: 19.5 tons.
Crew: 5.
Armament: one 76-mm M1A1 gun with 45 rounds and one .5-inch Browning M2 machine gun with 1,000 rounds.
Armour: hull front and sides 13-mm; turret front 19-mm, sides 13-mm, and mantlet 13-mm.
Engine: one Continental R-975 radial, 400-hp.
Speed: 45 mph.
Range: 150 miles.
Length: 17 feet 6 inches.
Height: 8 feet $4\frac{3}{4}$ inches.
Width: 9 feet $1\frac{1}{4}$ inches.

tired even to surrender.

"I left this area rather regretting I'd seen it . . . Under such conditions there are no supermen – all men become rabbits looking for a hole."

Most of the German *matériel* was lost. The French 2nd Armoured Division alone took 100 guns and 700 vehicles and the 90th Division 380 armoured vehicles, 700 guns, and more than 5,000 lorries.

Model succeeds Kluge

This was the situation which Field-Marshal Model inherited when he took over from Kluge at his H.Q. at Saint Germain-en-Laye on August 17. Two days previously a fortuitous incident had, if not provoked, at least hastened, the disgrace of Kluge. Whilst he was up at the front an aircraft bomb had demolished the radio truck which gave him permanent contact with O.K.W., and the ensuing prolonged silence caused Hitler

to conclude that C.-in-C. West had finally betrayed him and gone to see Montgomery about surrender terms.

Kluge's farewell to Hitler

When he said goodbye to his successor Kluge assured him that he would speak to Hitler with all the clarity which the situation demanded. But in the car taking him back to Germany he rightly persuaded himself that the dictator would give him, not an audience at O.K.W., but a criminal trial and an ignominious death. Potassium cyanide removed him from the Führer's vengeance, but before he committed suicide on August 18, 1944 he sent a letter to Hitler, the conclusion of which is worth recalling:

"I do not know if Field-Marshal Model who has proved himself in all respects will be capable of mastering the situation I hope so with all my heart. If that is not to be the case and if the new weapons—

especially air weapons, which you are so eagerly awaiting, are not to bring you success, then *mein Führer,* make up your mind to finish the war. The German people have endured such unspeakable sufferings that the time has come to put an end to their terrors. There must be ways to arrive at this conclusion and, above all, to prevent the Reich from being condemned to the hell of Bolshevism . . . *Mein Führer,* I have always admired your greatness and your iron will to assert your authority and uphold National Socialism. If your destiny overcomes your will and your genius, it will be because Providence has willed it so. You have fought a good and honourable fight. History will bear witness to this. If it ever becomes necessary, show yourself great enough to put an end to a struggle which has become hopeless."

We know what became of this advice from a man about to die: if it had been accepted Germany would have been spared, not the rigours of occupation (this had been decided at Teheran), but at least the appalling horrors of invasion.

Churchill again opposes a landing in Provence . . .

On the same August 15 when Army Group "B" was trying to escape from the Normandy net, the landing of an Allied force in Provence compelled O.K.W. for the first time to impose on the C.-in-C. West a withdrawal of considerable strategic importance. Right up to the last minute Churchill had tried to urge his American allies to abandon this operation, which was called first "Anvil" then "Dragoon", in favour of his projected offensive towards Vienna and the Danube across the Apennines, the Giulian Alps, and the Ljubljana gap.

In a letter dated August 6 to his friend Harry Hopkins, Churchill expressed his conviction that as the ports of Brest, Lorient, Saint Nazaire, and Nantes might fall into Allied hands "at any time", there was no logistic value left in Toulon or Marseilles. On the other hand, why not take the bull by the horns? "Dragoon", he wrote, would have to be carried out against an enemy who "at the outset [would] be much stronger than we are, and where our advance runs cross-grained

to the country, which abounds in most formidable rocky positions, ridges, and gullies."

"But", he noted in particular, "after taking the two fortresses of Toulon and Marseilles we have before us the lengthy advance up the Rhône valley before we even get to Lyons. None of this operation can influence Eisenhower's battle for probably ninety days after the landings."

. . . in favour of a campaign in the Balkans

On the next day he went to Portsmouth and saw Eisenhower about it, speaking his mind more openly than he had done to Hopkins, and not concealing his interest in a campaign in the Balkans, a subject which he had not broached in his letter. Eisenhower soon realised that the Prime Minister, in his opposition to "Dragoon", was putting forward reasons of strategy so as not to have to declare the political reasons which had made him take up this attitude.

Eisenhower's reserve

As a good American soldier General Eisenhower reckoned that he should not interfere in matters which were the responsibility of the White House and the State Department. He was to react the same way over Berlin later. He makes this perfectly clear in his memoirs when he says:

"Although I never heard him say so, I felt that the Prime Minister's real concern was possibly of a political rather than a military nature. He may have thought that a post-war situation which would see the western Allies posted in great strength in the Balkans would be far more effective in producing a stable post-hostilities world than if the Russian armies should be the ones to occupy that region. I told him that if this were his reason for advocating the campaign into the Balkans he should go instantly to the President and lay the facts, as well as his own conclusions on the table. I well understood that strategy can be affected by political considerations, and if the President and the Prime Minister should decide that it was worth while to prolong

△ △ *General Leclerc, holding the map board, follows the progress of his armoured division.*
△ *Lieutenant-General Omar N. Bradley, commander of the U.S. 12th Army Group.*

△ *The scene that was to greet the Allies when they reached the Seine: wholesale destruction, plus great dumps of ruined* matériel *such as this one at Rouen.*

the war, thereby increasing its cost in men and money, in order to secure the political objectives they deemed necessary, then I would instantly and loyally adjust my plans accordingly. But I did insist that as long as he argued the matter on military grounds alone I could not concede validity to his arguments."

And he was clearly right. The supreme commander may lay down strategic objectives, but it is the political leaders who set the aims of warfare. Moreover Churchill was too late. The drive for Vienna may have been conceivable on June 5 so long as everything was done to annihilate Kesselring south of the line Rimini–La Spezia, but it was not now, on August 7, by which time the enemy, whose

losses in retreat had not been overwhelming, was re-establishing his line along the ridges of the Apennines. At best the Allies would have been caught in late autumn on the narrow hemmed-in roads in the area of Klagenfurt or Ljubljana and have had to fight for peaks between 3,000 and 4,000 feet high. The mountainous terrain and the weather, to say nothing of enemy action, would have severely restricted all movement. Also, the nearest units of the American 12th Army Group, of which the forces used in this operation would have formed the right flank, had only got as far as Sombernon (20 miles west of Dijon) by September 12 and were changing direction northwards towards Chaumont and Epinal.

CHAPTER 128

Growth of the French Resistance

At noon on Monday, June 17, 1940, a young cadet at the Cavalry School at Saumur burst into the room where one of his officer-instructors was taking a hasty meal. The cadet seemed to be in a state of shock, and the breathless words with which he addressed the officer made no sense to the woman servant in the room. She looked on while the officer pushed back his chair, jumped to his feet, and strode to the door, wiping his eyes with the back of his hand as he went out.

Minutes before, the radio had broadcast a proclamation by Marshal Pétain which was to be repeated every hour until that evening:

"Frenchmen!"

"Called by the President of the Republic, I am taking over the direction of the government of France as from today.

"Certain of the devotion of our superb army, which is fighting with a heroism worthy of its long military tradition against an enemy superior both in numbers and in arms; certain that by its magnificent resistance it has fulfilled our duties to our allies; certain of the support of our old soldiers, whom I have been proud to command; certain of the confidence of the entire nation, I offer myself to France in order to lessen her suffering.

"It is with a heavy heart that I tell you

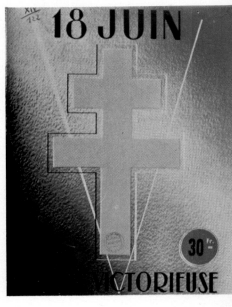

◄ "Whatever happens, the flame of French resistance must not be quenched and will not be quenched"–in the darkest hour of France's defeat in 1940 de Gaulle stood out as the natural focus for the resistance, both in France and abroad.
▽ Poster commemorating de Gaulle's electrifying broadcast of June 18, 1940.

1877

△ *De Gaulle in Britain,*
addressing the ship's company
of the Fighting French sloop
Commandant Duboc.

today that the fighting must cease. To-night I will contact the enemy and ask him if he is prepared to discuss with me, as between soldiers, after fighting the battle and defending our honour, the steps to be taken to end hostilities."

Twenty-four years before, the famous old soldier who made this announcement had galvanised the Verdun garrison with his immortal battle-cry *"Courage, on les aura!"*; and there can be no doubt that his heart was indeed torn by the need for France to lay down her arms in 1940. Those who heard him broadcast at the time still remember how his voice trembled as he concluded his speech. But as his words went out to the French people the roads of France were choked with countless refugees, haggard, desperate, swamping the fighting troops with their numbers and thus preventing any chance of a counter-attack, converting the retreat to a stampede on all sides. To take just one example, terrible scenes had occurred at the bridge at Gien, where nearly a million people had forced their way across the Loire in three days; and those scenes would be repeated as far afield as the Pyrenees and the Alps unless the fighting ended at once. Those who wanted to carry on the fight had to consider not only the chaotic state of the armies in the field. They could not ignore

the sufferings of those hundreds of thousands of women, children, and old folk who had travelled (for the most part on foot) from Holland, Belgium, and north-eastern France, pushing their pitiful bundles of possessions on barrows.

It is a grim fact that Pétain's premature announcement of his intention to request an armistice only added to the confusion and did nothing to alleviate the suffering of the civilian population. The Luftwaffe's Stukas and the Italian bombers continued to terrorise the floods of refugees streaming south, while Pétain's proclamation only troubled and demoralised the majority of the troops. Very few of them came to the decision that nothing would be changed until an armistice was actually signed, and that their duty was to fight on where they stood. Among these few were the officers and men at Saumur, whose stand on the banks of the Loire was one of the most heartening episodes in the overall tragedy of the 1940 campaign.

De Gaulle's reply

If Pétain's speech had not included that last paragraph, the people of France would have been immeasurably encouraged to hear that the man who had saved the French Army in 1917 and led it to victory in the following year had become their leader. But as it stood, it was a mistake, and in the prevailing conditions it prompted an immediate reply, for the good of France, which only led to more rivalry in the future.

This reply came on the following evening. Over the British radio came the voice of General de Gaulle, a generally unknown figure whose appointment three days before as Under-Secretary of State for National Defence had caused much surprise. Many a French officer regarded de Gaulle's initiative as a call to desertion. In fact it had the opposite effect: to proclaim to the world that France refused to accept that she had been decisively beaten. It was to de Gaulle's proclamation that France owed the right to join the victorious Allies at the conference table, to receive the surrender of Germany with an assurance which would have seemed insane in June 1940, with Germany victorious on all fronts. In his speech the day before, Pétain had paid tribute to the resistance of the French Army—too often discounted, despite the 100,000-odd deaths it had suffered since May 10. But de Gaulle gave the word "resistance" a new interpretation. "Whatever happens," he said, "the flame of French resistance must not be quenched and will not be quenched."

France can always be proud that these words were spoken by a Frenchman at a time when it seemed that all was lost. The flame lit by de Gaulle, however, spread to all countries under German occupation, and France was not the only country which would see the scrawled "V for Victory" sign combined with the Lorraine Cross, symbol of "Free France". De Gaulle's speech of June 18 was for the benefit of the whole of occupied Europe, and "resistance" would become the key rallying-cry against the common enemy.

De Gaulle's appeal was little understood at the time, and is often confused with the famous leaflet, bearing the tricolour flag, which appeared in London a few weeks later with the announcement beginning 'France has lost a battle, but France has not lost the war." What mattered was that the appeal existed. From its opening words Pétain – without being named – came under fire. "The commanders who have led the armies of France for many years have formed a government. This government has agreed with the enemy to end the struggle." On the following day de Gaulle's attack intensified: "Before

French minds are confused, before the dissolution of a government under enemy control...." And on June 22 the armistice was condemned in advance as "not a capitulation, but an enslavement".

Four days later de Gaulle, to his discredit, took up the word "enslavement" and flung it in Pétain's face. In so doing he created a breach which would have grave results for the destiny of France and was the source of unspeakable injustices and sufferings. The aggressive attitude he advocated was contrary to national opinion. The Parisians who would turn out to cheer de Gaulle on August 26, 1944, during his triumphal progress down the Champs Elysées, would nearly all be the same citizens who had greeted Pétain with equal fervour four months before on April 26, when he visited the occupied capital. Rouen, Dijon, Lyon, Nancy, and Epinal–the last being the closest Pétain got to Strasbourg, which the Germans forbade him to enter–and even Saint-Etienne, on D-Day itself, would welcome Pétain with the same infectious

▽ Opposite number to "Colonel Passy", head of de Gaulle's secret service: Colonel Maurice Buckmaster (standing, centre), head of the French section of Special Operations Executive.

enthusiasm.

Nearly all Frenchmen believed that there was a secret agreement between de Gaulle, who "took up the broken sword" on June 18, 1940, and the old Marshal, who at the same time used his personal aura to try and save his country from the excesses of the enemy. These Frenchmen believed vaguely that the welfare of France demanded unity, and they were right. All the evidence shows that Pétain did indeed "resist" in every sense of the word, and that his sentence by a vengeful court in August 1945 for "dealings with the enemy" was a grave miscarriage of justice for Pétain and for France.

De Gaulle's resistance

The resistance inspired and led by de Gaulle was different. Several former members of the "Free French" have argued that active resistance to the Germans would have existed in France without de Gaulle. This is true: acts of sabotage and attacks on German officers and soldiers were carried out by men who had not followed de Gaulle's lead. But the fact remains that without de Gaulle, resistance would have taken another form—and France would have been lost.

Everyone knows of the achievements

◁ ◁ *"The* Franc-Tireurs et Partisans *of France have poured out their blood for the people of Paris." A Communist resistance network, the "F.T.P." was nevertheless prepared to co-ordinate its activities with the other organisations in the field.*

AVIS

En vue d'inciter la population à entrer dans les groupes de résistance, les puissances ennemies tentent de répandre dans le Peuple Français la conviction que les membres des groupes de résistance, en raison de certaines mesures d'organisation et grâce au port d'insignes extérieurs, sont assimilés à des soldats réguliers et peuvent de ce fait se considérer comme protégés contre le traitement réservé aux francs-tireurs.

A l'encontre de cette propagande il est affirmé ce qui suit :

Le Droit International n'accorde pas, aux individus participant à des mouvements insurrectionnels sur les arrières de la Puissance Occupante, la protection à laquelle peuvent prétendre les soldats réguliers.

Aucune disposition, aucune déclaration des puissances ennemies ne peuvent rien changer à cette situation.

D'autre part, il est stipulé expressément, à l'article 10 de la Convention d'Armistice Franco-Allemande que les ressortissants français qui, après la conclusion de cette Convention, combattent contre le REICH ALLEMAND, seront traités par les troupes allemandes comme des francs-tireurs.

La puissance occupante, maintenant comme auparavant, considérera, de par la loi, les membres des groupes de résistance comme des francs-tireurs. Les rebelles tombant entre leurs mains ne seront donc pas traités comme prisonniers de guerre, et seront passibles de la peine capitale conformément aux lois de la guerre.

DER OBERBEFEHLSHABER WEST

◁ *Grim warning from the Germans—a public announcement in Paris: "In order to persuade the population to join resistance groups, the enemy powers are trying to convince the people of France that members of resistance groups, by virtue of certain organisational measures and the wearing of insignia, have the status of regular soldiers and may therefore consider themselves protected from the treatment reserved for terrorists.*

"In view of this propaganda the following is announced:

"International Law does not grant to individuals taking part in subversive activity within the territory of the Occupying Power, the protection which regular soldiers may claim.

"No resolution or declaration made by the enemy powers can change this situation.

"Moreover, Article 10 of the Franco-German Armistice Convention expressly states that French nationals who take up arms against the German Reich after the conclusion of that Convention, will be treated by German troops as terrorists.

"The occupying power considers and will continue to consider members of resistance groups as terrorists. Rebels falling into their hands will not be treated as prisoners of war and will be liable to the capital penalty in accordance with the conventions of war."

1881

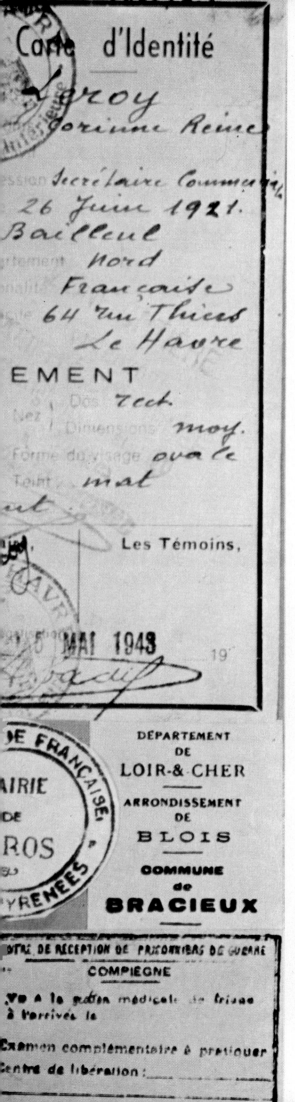

of the French Foreign Legion, but consider the case of the detachment in the Cameroons. Apart from its commander, Captain Danjou, and his two subordinate officers, very few of its number were Frenchmen. Its establishment was made up of Swiss, Belgians, Spaniards, Danes, Bavarians, Prussians, Württembergers, and Poles. Their achievement did not add to the battle honours of their original countries, but to the glory of France. And without de Gaulle's appeal of June 18, 1940, those men who crossed the Channel to carry on the fight in uniform would have been unable to do more than form a volunteer foreign legion which would have been part of the British Army. Without de Gaulle no Frenchman could have claimed, as de Gaulle himself persistently claimed, two years later: "The nation has thrilled with pride on hearing what its soldiers have achieved at Bir Hakeim—brave and true sons of France, who have written one of the most glorious pages in her history with their blood!"

The London organisation

As for myself, I had a better chance than others of crossing to England after the collapse in 1940. I was at my home in Brittany. Sheer instinct drove me to set out with my youngest brother on the morning of June 18. As I said to my wife: "If the Nazis win this war we will not only become their slaves, but the spirit of our children will be perverted, for they will be brought up under National Socialist principles." Not that I had a clear goal; the following evening found me at Verdon harbour, pleading in vain with the commander of a minesweeping sloop to take us to Morocco.

But a few days later, having been landed at Falmouth by a Norwegian ship, we gave in our names in a basement office near St. James's Palace, where "the man of June 18" had just set up his headquarters. Our particulars were recorded on a writing pad by a young second-lieutenant just returned from Narvik, and I heard that de Gaulle had had to pay for the pad out of his own pocket, his current finances being negligible. My spirits soared. I do not know of any great moral venture which has been launched with a full treasury, or with financial backing. We were there to defend the Christian idea of mankind as best we could, and as

◁ A selection of forged forms and stamps used by agents. They include French and Dutch municipalities, birth certificates, police and forced labour offices, and Wehrmacht and Gestapo stamps. There are also forged signatures of S.S. and other officials. The identity card in the name of "Corinne Reine Leroy" was carried by the British agent Violette Szabo.

long as we were poor all would be well. I felt already that we would win.

Shortly afterwards, however, I was being entertained with lavish hospitality by some British friends in a fine country house. I could not help wondering if I had been right to leave my family to the mercies of an enemy portrayed by the British press as acting with a total lack of pity towards occupied territory; and I looked around for a way of rejoining them without breaking my new undertaking. Finally I thought I found the answer in volunteering for a mission in France, although I knew nothing even of the most elementary facts of a secret agent's job. If I had had the least idea I would have realised that the plan would only have put those whom I wished to protect in greater danger.

My application was received by a young captain who went by the pseudonym of "Passy", which he had taken from a Parisian *métro* station in imitation of the first French volunteers, who came from the Narvik expeditionary corps. Lacking officers—as he then lacked everything else!—de Gaulle had put him in charge of the 2nd, 3rd, 4th, and 5th Bureaux of his skeletal staff; and although my military experience was very limited I thought that this was too much for one man to handle. Barely past his 30th birthday,

André Dewavrin was a brilliant officer, although quite inexperienced in his new functions.

He asked me to leave him my passport, however; and an examination of its pages with its Spanish stamps, suggested to his contacts in the Intelligence Service that I could be sent to France without much trouble. So it was that in early August I set out for Lisbon in a comfortable flying-boat. My secret agent's gear consisted only of a very simple code, which I carried in my head; a small bottle of invisible ink, which I never used at all; and 20,000 francs, which Passy had scraped together with some trouble. My mission was to report on German movements between the Spanish frontier and Mont Saint-Michel, through Brest. From my complete ignorance on how to collect such information, let alone pass it on, one would have thought that my zone extended to Scandinavia. To my tentative request for a radio transmitter, the British replied that their own army (still re-equipping after Dunkirk) had priority.

The growth of the network

Two years later, my network—which I had christened the *Confrérie Notre-Dame*—

continued on page 1889

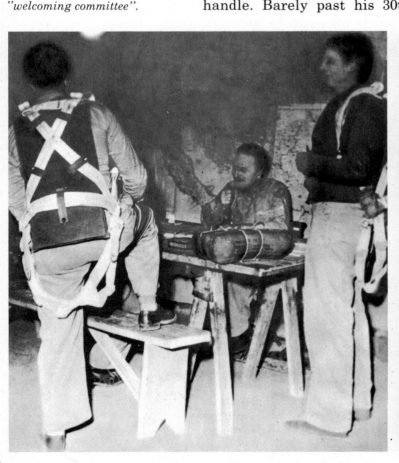

▽ Agents prepare for a mission to occupied France.
▽ ▷ Dropping supplies.
▷ ▷ A "body" arrives, photographed by one of the "welcoming committee".

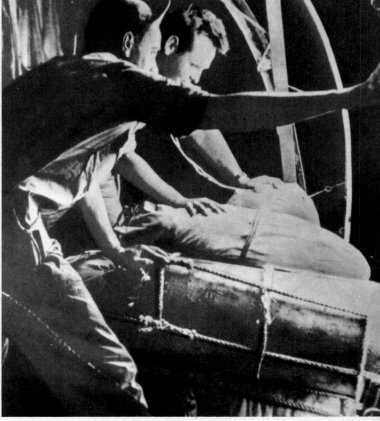

Ree, Captain Harry. *Known to the resistance as "Henri". Operated first in Jura region, setting up resistance networks. Organised sabotage of Peugeot motor works at Sochaux, oil tanks of the Usines Marti, and Leroy Machine Company factory at St. Suz. Network betrayed by French double agent. Constantly hunted and forced to take refuge in Switzerland. November 27, 1944, badly wounded in fight with Gestapo man. Sheltered and nursed by resistance; returned to London in July 1944 via Switzerland and Spain.*

Sansom, Odette. *Known to the resistance as "Lise". Operated in south of France as courier for Peter Churchill's network. Moved to St. Jorioz in the Savoy mountains with Churchill posing as his wife. Arrested with Churchill after their network was penetrated by the brilliant Abwehr counterspy agent, Hugo Bleicher. Tortured to supply information on other members of the Churchill network, but survived. Deported to Ravensbrück, but lived.*

Churchill, Captain Peter. *Known to the resistance as "Michel". First mission February 1942, delivering money to networks in south. Second mission delivering radio operators. August 1942, back to south of France to organise networks; forced to move from Cannes to Toulouse after German occupation. Shifted headquarters to St. Jorioz in Savoy mountains; arrested with Odette Sansom, April 1943. Survived Flossenbürg and Dachau.*

Inayat Khan, Noon. *Known to the resistance as "Madeleine". Radio operator for "Prosper" network in Paris. Left virtually on her own after mass Gestapo round-up in June-July 1943. Betrayed by woman informer and arrested. Shot at Dachau, September 1944.*

Dufour, Jacques. *Known to the Resistance as "Anastasie". maquis leader. Called "the biggest bandit in the Limoges region" by Germans. String of daring and successful sabotage actions. June 1944, set out to prevent S.S. "Das Reich" Panzer Division from moving north to Normandy. Operating with Violette Szabo, narrowly escaped capture when ambushed by S.S. at Salon-le-Tour. Continued operations against "Das Reich"; linked up with advancing Allies.*

Szabo, Violette. *Known to the resistance as "Corinne". Penetrated prohibited coastal zone and reconnoitred Rouen area, April 1944. Second mission in June (D+1), to work with maquis in the Limoges area. Captured after two-hour gun battle with "Das Reich" troops, allowing "Anastasie" to escape. Shot at Ravensbrück, January 1945.*

◁ *The Belgian resistance worker Françoise Labouverie, seen at far left disguised as "Nicole Desmanets" in February 1944. The two pictures were taken at about the same time.*

One agent's story

rançoise Labouverie was 20 hen Belgium was invaded in May 1940. She and her family ere swept up in the flood of efugees which fled from the Ger- an advance. They first headed or the coast at Dunkirk, and nally made for St. André in outhern France, via Rouen and ordeaux, where they stayed ith a friend of Madame Labou- erie for the next three months.

Then came the return to ccupied Belgium. Françoise pent the winter of 1940-41 in an ffice job in Brussels until ill ealth forced her to go home to éroux. Her mother decided to onvert their home to a guest ouse, and there Françoise made er first contact with resistance: e black market, maintained y the farming community.

In March 1941 Françoise ecame engaged, having heard at her fiancé was planning to scape to England. As the sum- er of 1941 wore on her deter- ination to escape as well ardened. She planned two train- g journeys: a bicycle trek rough the Ardennes and a ski- g holiday in the Jura. But ght tedious months of waiting assed before the first chance of scape materialised.

Via an old friend from her days as a Wolf Cub leader, Françoise met "Etienne", who gave her a message to deliver in the south of France. "You will go to Car- cassonne and on the third floor of the fifth house on your left in the Market Street, as you come from the market, you will find Madame Ladinde. Tell her Etienne and Paulette send their love–they remember the fireside chats. Tell her Hibou is holding on."

Françoise chose St. André as the point from which to attempt the tricky crossing of the de- marcation-line. Escorted across into Vichy France by a seasoned *passeur,* she headed for Lyon, where her cousin Jacques was attaché to the U.S. Embassy. She delivered her message to Madame Ladinde in Car- cassonne, and, back in Lyon, met "Oncle Roger", who was to escort her across the frontier into Spain. But it was not to be. She was turned back at the frontier, and began to work as secretary to "Oncle Roger".

Her work consisted mainly of copying maps and reports, "mainly concerning airports and landing fields in Belgium". But this phase ended abruptly when

the Germans marched into Vichy France on November 11, 1942. "Oncle Roger" flew to Algiers– taking Françoise's passport with him. She spent a month caring for the five children of a Belgian family, then made two more attempts to cross into Spain. But these, too, failed; Françoise knew that the longer she stayed in southern France she was risk- ing herself and her contacts there –and so she set off for Belgium again, arriving home at the end of December 1942.

As soon as possible she went to Brussels, looking for "Etienne", and agreed to work for him. "Etienne"–his real name was Pierre Hauman, a former captain of Belgian cavalry–had been running a small Intelligence *réseau* (network) for a year. It was called "Tegal"; the story went that when "Etienne" was asked to coin a cover-name for his group he had answered *"Ca m'est égal!"* ("It's all the same to me!") and the name stuck.

"Tegal" was a small and com- pact group: "Etienne" and his assistant Franz, the radio opera- tor, Bob, and Françoise as secre- tary formed the hard core. They passed on the reports of innumer- able agents; "you found them all

over Belgium, eager, courageous, selfless, they knew no one and asked no questions."

Known as "Nicole" in the "Tégal" *réseau,* Françoise was called upon to make many hazardous trips through occupied Belgium to contact agents. In the rented Brussels flat which served as the "Tégal" office, she typed lists of information, copied sketches, and helped while the information was put on micro- film before being conveyed to England. Then, on September 23, 1943, "Etienne" was betrayed and arrested. The "Tégal" members dispersed and went underground.

Françoise spent nine months on the wanted list, moving from address to address and existing with the help of relatives and friends, before her turn came. On June 13, 1944 she was arrested by the Rexists, Belgian quislings collaborating with the Germans. Held in St. Giles prison, she was interrogated by the Rexists and the Germans and was swept up with the other inmates of St. Giles on the approach of the Allied armies. They were en- trained for Germany–but sabo- tage by railway workers kept the train in Belgium; the prisoners were liberated on September 2.

◁ *An English radio receiver-transmitter specially designed for the Resistance. Radio operators in the field ran the constant risk of capture; the Germans operated radio-detection vans to track down intercepted transmissions to their source.*

▷ *Two years later (1943) than the model above, and much more compact: a pocket receiver used by resistance workers in the south of France.*

continued from page 1884

covered the whole of occupied France and Belgium, proving that Passy had been right and the experts of the British Intelligence Service wrong. The latter had put their faith in a long-term training programme for candidates like myself, using special schools, before putting the fully-trained agents "in the field". Passy replied to this by arguing that the war moved fast, and the conditions awaiting us in France did not match up with classic theories of espionage. Working in our own country, we would be able to count on the help of innumerable Frenchmen whom the Germans had been obliged to leave at their posts: in government departments, the railways, the ports, and the factories. Our agents, claimed Passy, would be able to use these Frenchmen to amass quantities of information which no agent working in a foreign country would otherwise be able to obtain—and, what was vital, to do it without delay and relay it back to headquarters at top speed.

Passy's views were correct. Between December 1940, when I sent him my first despatch (a very slim package, containing the vaguest of information), and the beginning of November 1943, when a betrayal virtually annihilated my network, we sent nearly 80 agents back to London. They were crammed with information—military, political, and economic—which often proved to be of the highest value, and carried bundles of scale drawings and maps and a good thousand radio messages. By this time, the end of 1943, Passy was a colonel, the head of the B.C.R.A. or *Bureau de contre-espionnage, de renseignements et d'action*. He gave me the job of setting up the *Section du Courrier Militaire*. I had daily to circulate between the various French and Allied services based in London some 10,000 roneoed reports, 3,000 photocopy sketches, and 500 photographs, some of which were often collages. To read, classify, collate, compile, reproduce, and distribute the incoming material from occupied France, I had the services of 120 skilled and keen volunteers who worked with me in the vast offices allocated to me in Palace Street. This was quite an advance from July 1940, when I had first entered Passy's modest office in St. Stephen's House, furnished as it was with nothing more than a plain wooden table and a couple of benches! Here, surely, was proof that above everything else the resistance was a matter of faith as well as of material resources.

Areas of operation

At the time of the armistice France had been divided into two zones, separated by an official "demarcation line". An appendix to the armistice convention defined this line with considerable precision; but in fact it was only settled after discussion between the districts directly involved, with the delimitations being settled on the spot. It is doubtful that the Germans had the last word. They did make some subsequent adjustments to the demarcation line in agreement with the local French authorities, but never got themselves involved in territorial squabbles. Nor was "The Line" the only frontier arbitrarily imposed on French territory. On August 7, 1940, a decree from Hitler annexed Alsace to the *Gau* of Baden in the Reich; and on November 30 of the same year Lorraine was proclaimed the *Gau Westmark* and annexed to the Third Reich in its turn.

The Germans imposed yet another zone. Its western limit ran from the Somme estuary through Abbeville, Amiens, Soissons, and Laon, meeting the "demarcation line" south of Dôle. This area came under the authority of General von Falkenhausen, Military Commander of Holland, Belgium, and northern France, who had his headquarters at Brussels. Stretching south to the Rhône at its exit from Lake Geneva, this zone was curiously similar to the western province of the original Holy Roman Empire; one German officer of the garrison at Salins-les-Bains in the Jura had declared: "We will reconstruct Lotharingia." This immense area of French territory the Germans called the "Green Zone"; it would be detached from France when final victory was won by the Reich. The French called it the "forbidden zone", for German control was stricter there than elsewhere; and especially along the Channel coast, which was known as the "Red Zone" in London. These refinements did not affect resistance workers in the Unoccupied Zone, whose preoccupations were very different. Their resistance took a political form, with the Vichy régime as its prime target. As for the Germans, they were only a secondary problem in the south—until the occupation of November 1942.

These differing attitudes soon hardened the demarcation line into a real frontier. In occupied France it became possible to

continued on page 1894

Gestapo terror...Firing-squad...

More than any other organ of the Nazi state, the Gestapo won international notoriety as the most feared and efficient instrument of Hitler's "New Order". Like the S.S., however, the Gestapo could never have earned this reputation if it had merely consisted of brutal thugs. In fact it was staffed with brilliant and ruthless detectives whose brainwork was devoted to tracking down the enemies of the state.

Its full style and title was *Geheime Staatspolizei* – Secret State Police – and it was as old as the Nazi state itself. Göring established the Gestapo in Prussia on April 26, 1933, months before the death of Hindenburg and Hitler's accession to total power over the Reich. From the start its task was a witch-hunt against all opponents of the Party and the régime. It was deeply involved in the Reichstag fire and the crushing of Röhm's S.A. Fear of the Gestapo was instrumental in securing the massive *"Ja"* plebiscite votes which strengthened Hitler's hold on Germany and Austria. But as the 1930s drew on it became apparent that the Gestapo's rôle as a direct instrument of state power had hardly begun.

Typical of this was the Nazi attempt to charge General von Fritsch, commander-in-chief of the Army, with homosexual offences. It was the Gestapo who found the unsavoury figure of Hans Schmidt, who trailed a long record of blackmailing homosexuals, to swear that he had caught Fritsch *flagrante delicto* in a Berlin back alley with an underworld character who rejoiced in the title of "Bavarian Joe". The Army won one of its last victories over the régime when Fritsch was cleared in a court of honour – but the Gestapo escaped from the whole depressing affair without being indicted in turn, although it had been caught out in an attempted perversion of justice of almost farcical dimensions.

When the time came for Hitler's invasion of Poland, the Gestapo was in the forefront. Heinrich Müller, its chief, was ordered to provide convicted criminals for an operation known as "Canned Goods". A party of Germans,

dressed in Polish uniforms, were to raid the German radio station at Gleiwitz, make a rapid broadcast, fire a few shots, and vanish, leaving the body of a uniformed "Pole" for discovery by the outraged Germans. This was duly done and the whole affair trumpeted to the world as the last Polish act of aggression which Germany would ever have to tolerate.

With the coming of the war the Gestapo's activities radiated out into the occupied territories, hunting down Jews and resistance leaders. No less than the Stuka and the Panzer division, it was an instrument of war, to root out resistance at source and keep enemy populations cowed by the terror of its name.

As the French Resistance grew in confidence and stature, so the Gestapo was forced to refine its tactics. One of the most successful counter-espionage *coups* in the story of the French resistance was achieved not by the Gestapo itself but by Sergeant Hugo Bleicher of the *Abwehr,* who used the terror of the Gestapo's name to induce captured agents and resistance workers to co-operate with the Germans. By passing himself off as a Luftwaffe officer who had decided that Germany had lost the war, and that he wanted to go over to the Allies, Bleicher later managed to penetrate Peter Churchill's resistance network based on St. Jorioz in the Savoy Alps and destroy it, adding to his laurels with the arrest of Churchill and Odette Sansom.

It was the work of expert counterspies such as Bleicher which made the task of the Gestapo much easier than it would otherwise have been in France. The Gestapo was more than willing to work with its military counterparts – the *Feldpolizei* and the *Abwehr.* The subtlety used to track down the key men in the resistance was taken to considerable extremes. But once an arrest had been made the subtlety ended.

Brute force was the basic

1. *Awaiting their next victims: splintered firing-posts in a bullet-pocked cellar in Paris.*
2-5. *Grim sequence of German photographs record the last seconds of a resistance worker in Paris. The numbers on the back wall make the yard a horrible parody of a shooting-range.*

...and torture chamber

method employed on Gestapo prisoners. For a start, the Gestapo knew very well that if an arrested agent could hold out for 48 hours his contacts would have time to disperse and a general alert sounded in the local resistance network. Speed was therefore of the essence.

A Gestapo interrogation had a standard, no-nonsense opening to show the victim that he was utterly in the power of his tormentors: two or more men at work on him at once, slaps, punches, kicks, and abuse, until the victim slumped on the edge of his chair on the verge of unconsciousness. He would then be revived and as likely as not subjected to a period of "soft" treatment – his handcuffs loosened, a cigarette offered and lit, coffee and food provided. But this phase could not be unduly protracted because it gave the victim time to recover and build up his strength to face the next onslaught.

The next phase would redouble the ferocity of the first. In the case of Yeo-Thomas, the "White Rabbit", it consisted of being stripped naked and hustled into a bathroom where a chain was wrapped round his ankles. He was then thrown into the bath which was full of icy water and his feet were hoisted out of the water, plunging his head beneath the surface. Despite his struggles he was held in that position until he passed out; he was then hauled out, given artificial respiration to bring him round, and the process repeated again and again.

In the case of Yeo-Thomas this was then followed by being hoisted from the ground by his hands, which were manacled behind his back, until his shoulders were dislocated and he passed out again. This in turn was followed by a terrifying beating with rubber coshes, including his genitals. Holding out against all these appalling tortures, Yeo-Thomas finally convinced the Gestapo that he was a hopeless case. He was sent to Germany for extermination, but escaped from Buchenwald.

Only against men and women of the calibre of Yeo-Thomas did the terror brutality of the Gestapo fail. But when it did it was found that the failure was total.

7

6-7. *There was nothing subtle about the way the Gestapo went to work. They were out to get confessions and information in the shortest possible time and they brought the art of physical torture to a pitch unheard-of since the days of the Inquisition. And with the benefits of 20th Century civilisation they were able to use a particularly horrible form of persuasion: electrocution.*
6. *Suspended on these contacts the victim would jerk in helpless agony while the current flowed.*
7. *Testament of anguish: human hand-marks scoured in the wet concrete of a cellar wall. The victims would be shoved into the cellar, the concrete would be soaked to improve the electrical contact – and the current would then be turned on . . .*

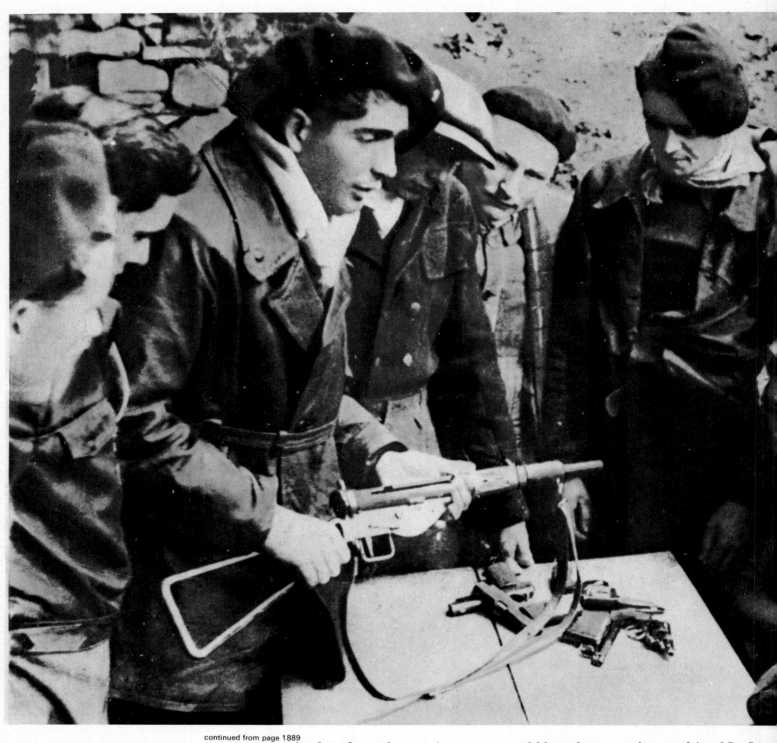

△ *Sten gun instruction in the field. The Sten was an ideal weapon for resistance work: tough, easy to operate, and simple to dismantle for concealment purposes.*

continued from page 1889

sense an attitude of condescension towards compatriots in the *"zone nono"*. This was unjust, but certainly resistance in southern France did not become effective before the Germans took over in November 1942. But there were compensatory factors. As from February 27, 1942, when one of the very first successful air supply missions was accomplished, the Unoccupied Zone was an invaluable help in getting our information back to London. Contained in a parcel whose contents would be unknown to the bearer, our message would be entrusted to the guard of the Pau-Canfranc train. At Canfranc it would be taken over by our friend Le Lay controller of customs, who would send it on to Jacques Pigeonneau, French Ambassador in Madrid. Pigeonneau would then deposit it in our "letter-box", represented by a British commercial traveller in Madrid. By diplomatic pouch it would then be passed on to Lisbon and flown back to London. We had no mishaps although the system had its risks, but it was very slow; and the same went for messages sent out by Passy from London. This was the route by which, at the beginning of 1941, I finally received my long-awaited radio transmitter, which

German counter-measures

Until the end of 1941 the main contribution of the French resistance was not acts of sabotage but the steady flow of sketched Intelligence matter. The German reaction was swift and severe. I can remember a poster, dated August 29, 1941, displayed in the *métro*. It announced the execution of Commander d'Estienne d'Orves, Maurice Barlier, and Jan Doornik, all three of them shot "for acts of espionage". Until I saw this poster I had not known their names. On October 24 it was the turn of my first radio operator, Bernard Anquetil, arrested at Saumur three months before, who had refused to save himself by betraying me. Like the other three he was shot at Mont-Valérien. The same fate was suffered by Charles Deguy on July 29, 1942. Deguy was the "number two" of my friend Maurice Duclos, known to the resistance as "Saint-Jacques", whose mission had preceded mine by a few days. Five names; five typical examples of sacrifice. At least they died under the bullets of a firing-squad and were spared the long agony of the camps.

After the outbreak of the Russo-German war on June 22, 1941, the effective strength of the Resistance in occupied France grew at such a speed that it caused us much suspicion at first. We had no way of knowing that the Communist Party would throw in its lot with the common cause. It did, at least in theory, put its French *Francs-Tireurs et Partisans* (F.T.P.) under de Gaulle's authority, in a letter written at the end of 1942 which I took to London together with Fernand Grenier, a member of the Party Central Committee. The superb courage of the men and women of the F.T.P. overcame many initial suspicions, although many of them could never reconcile their own beliefs with the Communist ideal. Yet the F.T.P. was not prevented by Communism from fighting and dying for France, and they should not be confused with the thugs and bandits who called themselves F.T.P. after their territory was liberated. In 1941 the F.T.P. concentrated on "action" planning – sabotage and attacks against the Germans – rather than on pure Intelligence work. The tight control of the Party slowed down the flow of information so much that it frequently lost its highest value.

In 1941 liberation seemed a very long way off, and hopes of insurrection against

rrived in a heavy and bulky suitcase. Our first radio contact with London was made from the house of Louis de La Bardonnie at Saint Antoine-de-Breuilh in the Unoccupied Zone, not far from the demarcation line cutting the road from Libourne to Sainte Foy-la-Grande. Shortly afterwards the transmitter was moved to Saumur, where it fell into the hands of the Germans at the end of July 1941. But in its brief career it had been instrumental in keeping the battle-cruisers *Scharnhorst* and *Gneisenau* immobilised in Brest, and thus, more remotely, in the destruction of the *Bismarck*.

he still formidable German occupation forces seemed impossible. The *maquis* was still a thing of the future (it was born of the refusal to obey the *Service de Travail Obligatoire*, the S.T.O. or "compulsory labour service", at the end of 1942). Yet optimistic and far-sighted leaders were already at work recruiting for the future, concentrating on men who would stick by their combat groups when the time came to come out into the open and fight weapon in hand.

Operational groups

Foremost among these groups was the *Organisation Civil et Militaire* (O.C.M.). In April 1942 its leader was Colonel Alfred Touny, who was shot with 12 of his comrades at Arras two years later. Then there were the *Chantiers de la Jeunesse*,

◁ ◁ *Hero of the hour – a* maquis *fighter in confident pose, cradling his Bren gun.*
△ *A* maquis *camp: weapon-cleaning time.*
◁ *The inner man. A* maquis *group toasts the coming of liberation.*

△ *Interrogation in the field: grilling a suspected collaborator.*

or "youth camps", which traced their origins back to June 2, 1940. On that day General de La Porte du Theil resigned the command of VII Corps and the War Ministry gave him the difficult and unenviable job of regrouping the young men called up in 1940, who were out on the roads in tens of thousands, living by looting. Given this unpleasant job, de La Porte du Theil saw in it a way of preserving the system of compulsory service and military instruction despite the very strict terms of the armistice, and Marshal Pétain backed him to the hilt. The title *Chantiers de la Jeunesse* was a blanket term to deceive the Germans. It took them a long time to find out what de La Porte du Theil was really doing; the Gestapo did not arrest him until January 4, 1944. Such was the confusion which accompanied the liberation that this veteran resistance worker was charged with collaboration with the Germans after his own liberation in Germany; but orders from the top saw the charge dismissed before any injustice could be done. Many of those who had been formed into *Chantiers de la Jeunesse* made up the framework of the *maquis*, and a large part of de Lattre de Tassigny's 1st

Army consisted of recruits from the *Chantiers* along the road from the south of France to Alsace–apart, that is, from those troops mobilised in North Africa. Only a short time was needed to train these young recruits–a matter of hours–and their conduct in action was superb. Finally, in the Vichy zone, there were the *Compagnons de la France* ("companions of France"). They played an important part in the liberation, and one of the most famous names in our network, *Georges Lamarque*, came from their ranks.

A brave gesture

On November 11, 1940, there was a brave demonstration in Paris which completely flouted the German occupation decrees. From morning to evening, despite brutal German counter-measures, thousands of students and schoolchildren (some of whom were not yet 15 years old) turned out to lay wreaths on the tomb of the Unknown Soldier at the Arc de Triomphe. Similar demonstrations took place in Brussels and Luxembourg.

Resistance outside France

Like Belgium, Luxembourg had endured four years of German occupation in World War I while Holland preserved her neutrality. This time, while King Léopold III declared himself a prisoner of the invaders of his country, Grand Duchess Charlotte and Queen Wilhelmina left their countries for London, from where they inspired their subjects to resist. Holland now had to begin learning the art of resistance which Belgium and Luxembourg had learnt 22 years before. As early as June 15, 1940, the citizens of Brussels and Liège—to the fury and consternation of the German occupation authorities—were circulating two subversive leaflets: *Ssh!* and *The World of Labour*. The Belgians were not content with this. When the Belgian Army surrendered, Major William Grisard had ended his last order of the day with words that heralded de Gaulle's later appeal to the French: "This is not the end. This is only a phase, and we will meet again." In the second fortnight of June, Brevet-Colonel Lentz, chief-of-staff of

the 17th Infantry Division, began to re-group the most reliable and determined men from the regiments of that division who had evaded captivity. At about this time Captain-Commandant Claser began to organise the "L.B." or *Légion Belge*. While Lentz concentrated on garrison towns for his recruiting, keeping his net-work essentially military, Claser took in civilians, with reservists and professional soldiers recruited on a regional basis.

By October 1940 the whole of Belgium had been organised into three zones and nine provinces, grouped in regions and sub-regions. Claser and Lentz worked to-gether, with Lentz retaining the military command. Claser, aided by Lieutenant van de Putte as head of information and by reserve Captain Boerenboom, acted as chief-of-staff to what eventually became

first the "Army of Belgium" and later the "Secret Army". The reserve units, organ-ised on a regimental basis, were com-manded by Brevet-Colonel Bastin, a World War I hero, and director of the Red Cross P.O.W. parcel service. In accordance with previous plans, Bastin took over the L.B. from Lentz when the latter was arrested on May 8, 1942. Claser was arrested and died in captivity. Lieutenant van der Putte and Captain Boerenboom were also rounded up. However, before his capture Lentz had succeeded in unifying the various elements of the Belgian resistance, forming a central committee under the presidency of Colonel Heenen, whose general secretary was Frans Bodaert, Lentz's liaison officer.

The geographical position of Holland, Belgium, and Luxembourg led to the early

△ *and* ▽ *The confidence of coming victory: formal parades.* ▷ *German counterblast to the resistance: a poster deploring the "terrorist" activities of captured and executed resistance workers in other occupied territories.*

DES LIBÉRATEURS?

GRZYWACZ
JUIF POLONAIS
2 ATTENTATS

ELEK
JUIF HONGROIS
8 DÉRAILLEMENTS

WASJBROT
JUIF POLONAIS
1 ATTENTAT - 3 DÉRAILLEMENTS

WITCHITZ
JUIF POLONAIS
15 ATTENTATS

FINGERWEIG
JUIF POLONAIS
3 ATTENTATS - 5 DÉRAILLEMENTS

BOCZOV
JUIF HONGROIS
CHEF DÉRAILLEUR
20 ATTENTATS

FONTANOT
COMMUNISTE ITALIEN
12 ATTENTATS

ALFONSO
ESPAGNOL ROUGE
7 ATTENTATS

MANOUCHIAN
ARMÉNIEN
CHEF DE BANDE
56
ATTENTATS
150 MORTS
600 BLESSÉS

RAYMAN
JUIF POLONAIS
13 ATTENTATS

LA LIBÉRATION!
PAR L'ARMÉE DU CRIME

appearance of a form of resistance which was only found in France along the approaches to the "forbidden zone" and the demarcation line. The first task was to conceal from the Germans those British servicemen who had failed to embark from Dunkirk. The close German watch on the North Sea coast made it too difficult to get the fugitives home by sea. It was therefore a matter of establishing, with the co-operation of the people of the French frontier zones, escape routes or "chains" whose links were gradually extended as far as the Pyrenees. These British escapers were immediately joined by Belgians who wished to carry on the fight in uniform. Soon there appeared, in their thousands, French escapers from German prison camps, who followed R.A.F. bomber crews shot down during missions over the Ruhr.

So many men and women devoted them-selves to helping the escapers that an accurate estimate count of their number is impossible. Two escape networks in Belgium deserve special mention, "Comet" and "Pat O'Leary". The latter was set up by Dr. Albert-Marie Guérisse. He was a Belgian Army surgeon who escaped at Dunkirk, returned to France to continue the struggle, was captured and escaped shortly after the armistice. Returning to France on a secret mission he was captured but escaped again, and set up one of the most important escape networks before being captured a third time and deported to Germany. "Comet" was formed by a girl, Andrée de Jongh, who had often heard the story of Edith Cavell's heroism in World War I from her father, a headmaster at Schaerbeek in the suburbs of Brussels. From strenuous personal efforts she built up an escape route from Belgium to Bilbao. She took

personal charge of her "children", cross-ing the Somme (often swimming, if neces-sary), taking them by train to Bayonne and into Spain by a hazardous mountain crossing. Andrée de Jongh was also arrested and deported. "Comet" paid a heavy price, but its efforts enabled almost a thousand airmen of the R.A.F. and U.S.A.A.F. to escape and fight again.

In Holland, Belgium, and Luxembourg, many ordinary houses concealed hundreds of French ex-P.O.W.s who had escaped from Germany. These men had to be hidden, fed, and provided with clothing and shoes – duties which were made almost impossible by the hard conditions of the occupation, and which raised the most difficult problems. Women resistance workers learned to bake bread in their own ovens; their menfolk learned how to butcher pigs and cattle. Fed and cared for – often provided with money saved by household economy – the prisoners would then be taken to another hiding place on the next stage of their journey to freedom,

▽ *Out in the open at last, to join forces with the Allies. Resistance fighters drive through Rheims beneath the tricolour.*
▷ ▷ ▽ *The ugly side of liberation. A policeman drags a beaten-up collaborator to captivity by his hair.*

gradually approaching the last barrier: the demarcation line. In this dangerous underground game, the Dutch, Belgian, Luxembourg, and French resistance workers, helped by priests, played a rôle of vital importance. With incredible self-sacrifice, ingenuity, and courage, they threw themselves into the task of conveying the fugitives into the Unoccupied Zone, despite the formidable advantages held by the Germans. The number of successful escapes ran into tens of thousands.

German vigilance and oppression bore down particularly hard on Luxembourg, considered by the invaders as part of the Fatherland which had been arbitrarily detached, and now to be thoroughly "Germanised". On the orders of Gauleiter Gustave Simon the slogan *"Heim ins Reich!"* (Home to the Reich!) was everywhere displayed. On August 30, 1942, Simon announced the compulsory call-up for the Wehrmacht of all Luxembourgers between the ages of 20 and 24. The reply of the people of Luxembourg was immediate and remarkable: a spontaneous general strike, which even saw teachers

and pupils staying away from their schools. The key centres were Wiltz in the north, and Esch in the south. It was a superb demonstration of how the Luxembourgers felt about the German intention to annex the Grand Duchy.

The grim year of 1941 ended with a dark and hard winter. Its gloom affected heart and soul, for it was clear that the war was still only in its opening phase. It would be many weeks and months before the first definite hope of liberation showed over the horizon, and then only at the price of untold sacrifice. The wife of one of my friends – one of the first recruits in my network – recently reminded me of how I replied to her fears of the risks her husband was running. I had told her, "But we are already all dead men!" In view of the losses already suffered and the dangers still to be run, it seemed impossible to me that any of us would escape with our lives. Why is it that many of us who did survive still feel nostalgia for those times when grief was second nature to us? The simple reason was that in the resistance there was no place for double-dealing, and we learned what confidence means when it has to be absolute. We depended totally upon each other and extended this sense of mutual loyalty to all our colleagues, even if they were not personally involved in what we happened to be doing.

This confidence gave us tremendous strength, for it allowed no compromise. When I heard that my radio operator Bernard Anquetil had been arrested, I had a moment's doubt. He knew the small flat where I lived; he had been there several times. And I knew what methods the Germans use to extract information from even the bravest men. But I could not help thinking that if my friend were to hear that I had quit my address, he would think that I had doubted his trustworthiness. I stayed where I was. And indeed Bernard Anquetil went before the firing squad without having told his interrogators of my whereabouts.

That, basically, was what made the opening phase of the Resistance so inspiring: the discovery of what life really meant, in the company of men and women inspired by the same ideal. We shared a common faith in the destiny of our country, and the much more intangible (but no less real) respect for the freedom and dignity of mankind. And those who lost their lives during the most hopeless phase of the struggle surely played the finest part.

Revenge on the collaborators

The story of the French resistance included a running fight between the agents and workers in the field and the German skill at using counterspies and double agents. These traitors had different motives. There was "Horace", a liaison agent dismissed by Yeo-Thomas, the "White Rabbit", for unpunctuality and mendacity. A weak and greedy young man, "Horace" became a double agent for the Gestapo and Yeo-Thomas had the grim satisfaction of unmasking him to the Germans at a confrontation after his arrest.

Then there was the case of "The Cat", radio operator for the *Interallié* network. This was another coup for the *Abwehr* ace, Hugo Bleicher. It began with the arrest of a section leader, Raoul Kiffer. Bleicher broke him down by telling him that his comrades had betrayed him, and Kiffer agreed to work for the Germans. On his information Mathilde Carré, "The Cat", was arrested in her turn. Bleicher gave her the full V.I.P. luxury treatment transferring her from jail to a hotel suite. He told her that he had all the information he needed to send all her comrades before a firing squad, and followed this up by telling her that if she helped him he could keep them out of the Gestapo's clutches and see that they were treated as prisoners-of-war. "The Cat" agreed. All the key members of *Interallié* were rounded up–and Bleicher prepared for the second phase of his plan, using "The Cat" to send bogus radio messages back to London as if the network were still intact, and so trap other agents. To begin with this was successful; but soon doubts began to creep in across the Channel. By the time that Bleicher took the bold step of sending "The Cat" back to England, suspicions were thoroughly aroused at S.O.E. and "The Cat" broke down and confessed on being taxed with being a double agent. But the damage she had done lived after her, and several agents were arrested by the Germans after her capture.

The Jura resistance had the problem of "the man who drove for the Gestapo", Pierre Martin, who gave the resistance much valuable help before being unmasked as a double agent. Harry Rée, chief S.O.E. agent in the Jura, made repeated attempts to settle accounts with Martin. The traitor was eventually gunned down by a vengeance *équipe* headed by Paul Simon, who caught Martin alone in a hotel restaurant in Besançon. Fate was not kind to Simon; he was trapped by an S.S. squad at the Café Grangier at Sochaux early in 1944 and died trying to shoot it out with the Germans.

Strangely, many of the "V-men"–as these double agents were known–often retained much of their loyalty towards their former employers and tried to shield them. Conversely, German counterspy aces such as Bleicher were as often as not fully aware that their tools were not giving them full information, but kept them on to add to their own knowledge. Thus, via Roger Bardet–who had been instrumental in the destruction of the St. Jorioz circuit – Bleicher made contact with network leader Henri Frager, and began to drop heavy hints that he "knew all". He nevertheless allowed Frager to return to England by Lysander, an act for which Bleicher was severely reprimanded by his superiors in *Abwehr*. Finally,

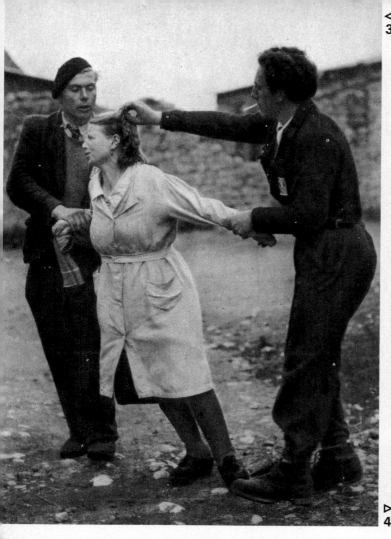

3

5

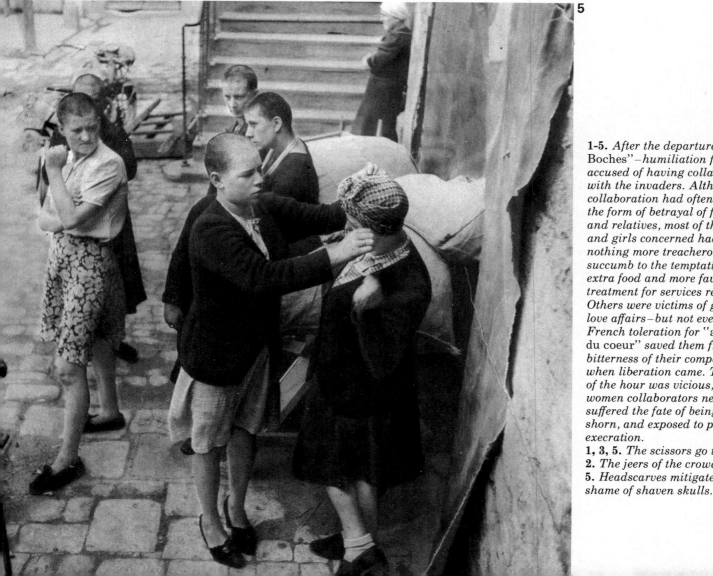

1-5. *After the departure of "Les Boches"—humiliation for women accused of having collaborated with the invaders. Although this collaboration had often taken the form of betrayal of friends and relatives, most of the women and girls concerned had done nothing more treacherous than succumb to the temptation of extra food and more favourable treatment for services rendered. Others were victims of genuine love affairs—but not even the French toleration for "affaires du coeur" saved them from the bitterness of their compatriots when liberation came. The mood of the hour was vicious, and women collaborators nearly all suffered the fate of being seized, shorn, and exposed to public execration.*

1, 3, 5. *The scissors go to work.*
2. *The jeers of the crowd.*
5. *Headscarves mitigate the shame of shaven skulls.*

1907

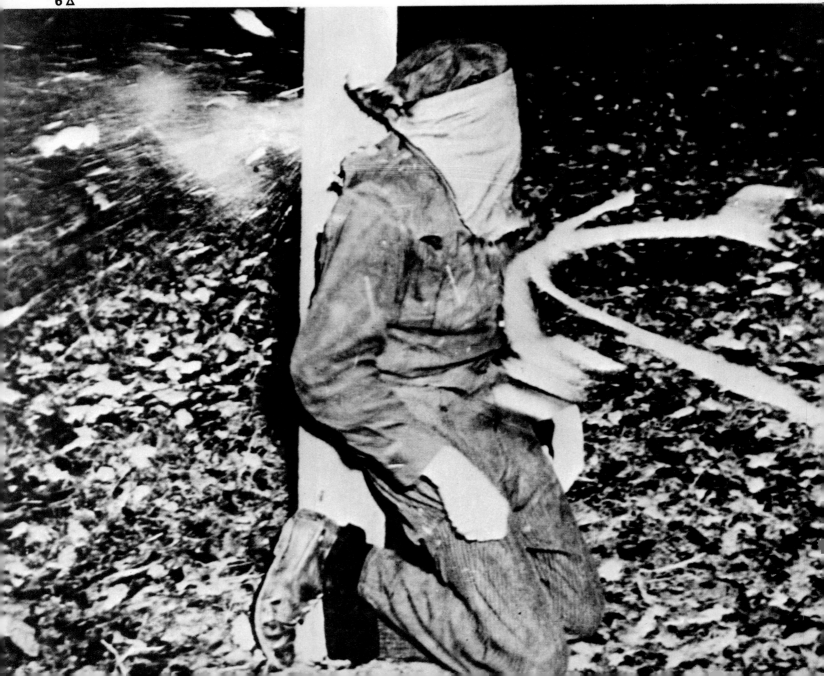

given a blunt ultimatum by the S.D. – the prompt arrest of Frager, or the ignominy of a People's Court trial – Bleicher found himself with no alternative but to put an end to Frager's activities. The Frenchman had genuinely believed in Bleicher's *bona ides;* Bleicher, in turn, had developed genuine respect for Frager's courage and patriotism. Bleicher's attempts to arrange fair treatment for Frager came to nothing; he died in Buchenwald concentration camp.

These are only a few of the many strange cases in the story of the resistance when personal concepts of treachery and loyalty became so enmeshed as to become almost indecipherable. It was a weird and paradoxical mixture; the heights of devotion to duty and the depths of personal self-seeking, a game played for mortal stakes in which the contestants made use of everything they could get their hands on to achieve their aim.

At the other end of the scale the people of the occupied territories had to live with collaboration of a more basic nature. This sprang from the basic human instinct to "beat the system", sharpened by the more immediate hardships of the occupation – shortage of food and comforts, the curfew, travel restrictions. Those Frenchmen who turned informer were very soon in need of German protection; there were many cases of stool-pigeons and spies being murdered. And it

was inevitable that there was little or no tolerance for women who slept with *"les Boches",* despite the traditional French respect for *affaires du coeur.*

With the coming of liberation the revenge taken on collaborators was savage. Men were beaten up by mobs and given scant attention by the authorities; women marked down as "Boche lovers" went through the humiliation of having their heads shaved and being paraded through the streets. This caused much concern to the British and American troops who witnessed these scenes; the standing order was on no account to get involved in how the French chose to settle their own accounts. But there were several cases of Allied officers intervening and stopping the shaving of old women whose daughters and relatives had been judged guilty, or even those who were considered to have shown insufficient distaste at having troops billeted in their homes.

The two most prominent Frenchmen to be accused when their country was liberated were, of course, the Vichy leaders, Pétain and Laval. Few tears were shed over Laval, who had always been the most outspoken collaborator of them all. But Pétain's case was a tragic one, proving the shortness of men's memories and the fragility of their gratitude.

In 1916 Pétain had saved Verdun and become a national hero; in the following year, when General Nivelle's offensive on the

Chemin des Dames completely broke the French Army's morale, it was Pétain who picked up the pieces and restored morale. By 1940 he stood out as the Grand Old Man of French military tradition and glory. But what he had seen in World War I had had a fatal effect on his outlook. During the bloody struggle for Verdun his watchword had been "one does not fight with men against *matériel";* by 1940 he was determined that at all cost France must be spared from needless suffering, and that it was his duty to see that this was done. Widely respected in France during the war – he was given enthusiastic welcome in many major French cities – he suddenly appeared in 1945 as the *capitulard* of 1940.

He faced his trial with dignity, wearing a plain uniform with no decorations apart from the *Médaille Militaire* and refusing to take his baton into court – "that would be theatrical." Condemned to death (the sentence was later commuted to life imprisonment), Pétain accepted the verdict stoically. His humiliation extended to having his name chopped out from the head of the Roll of Honour at Verdun. He died in 1951.

Pétain's sentence was typical of the cruel and vengeful mood at work in France after the war. And his tragedy was summed up by one of his *aides-de-camp:* "You think too much about the French and not enough about France."

The firing squad for collaborators sentenced to death.
6. *A mass execution.*
7. *Death of a traitor. His bonds are flying loose, sliced by the bullets.*
Overleaf: *A poster honouring the F.F.I.* – Forces Françaises de l'Intérieur. *It reflects the pride felt towards the resistance fighters as the "home army" of France.*

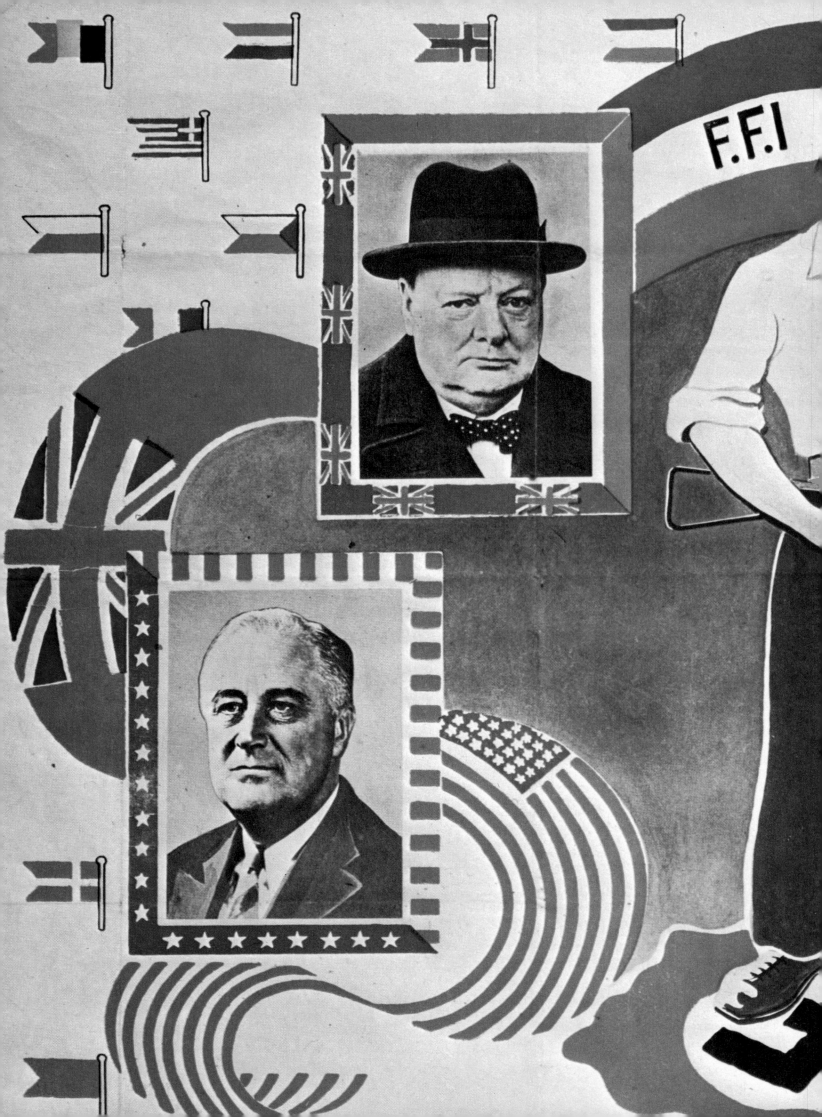

F.F.I

URSS

URSS

CHAPTER 129

DRAGOON:
The drive through southern France

Operation "Dragoon", supervised by General Maitland Wilson, C.-in-C. Mediterranean, was to be the landing between Saint Raphael and le Lavandou of the American 7th Army under Lieutenant-General A. M. Patch, who the previous year had been so successful in cleaning up Guadalcanal. The landing operation was to be carried out by the American VI Corps with its 3rd, 36th, and 45th Divisions, well experienced in amphibious operations. It was to be supported by an Anglo-American parachute division under Major-General Robert T. Frederick landing in the area of le Muy with the object of opening up the Argens valley. A position nearer Toulon was not chosen because of the danger of the two twin turrets at Cap Cépet whose guns could hurl a 119-pound shell a distance of nearly 22 miles.

A thousand ships were required: warships, troop transports, and supply vessels. These included five battleships, nine escort carriers (216 aircraft), 24 cruisers, 122 destroyers and escort vessels, and 466 landing craft, all from five navies: American, British, Australian, French, and Greek. The fleet, named the Western Task Force, was commanded by Vice-Admiral H. Kent Hewitt. On board his flagship was James Forrestal, the new U.S. Navy Secretary.

Air support came from the U.S. 12th Air Force, under Brigadier-General Gordon P. Saville, with 2,100 aircraft. Its heavy bombers operated from the area of Rome, its medium bombers, fighter-bombers, and fighters from 14 airstrips which had been built in the Bastia area. Any objectives out of range of the latter would be dealt with by carrier-based aircraft under Rear-Admiral T. H. Troubridge, R.N. On August 13 and 14, the four-engined bombers prepared the way for the landings by attacking gun-emplacements, communication centres, bridges, and viaducts. These attacks were spread over an area from Port-Vendres to Genoa to deceive the enemy.

The German defences

The defence of the 400 miles of coastline between Menton and Cerbère was the responsibility of the German 19th Army.

◁ ◁ *A French Sherman splashes ashore in Provence.*
▽ *American transport speeds the advance to the north.*

△ Build-up. Massed vehicles in Italy, earmarked for "Dragoon".
▷ ▷ △ On the way. Part of the impressive task force which screened the armada.
▷ ▷ Closing the beaches.

On D-day it had six divisions, deployed with three on each side of the Rhône. Between June 6 and August 4 it had had to give up its 217th, 272nd, and 277th Divisions, receiving in exchange only the 198th and the remnants of the 716th, which had been thrashed at Caen. Colonel-General Blaskowitz, C.-in-C. Army Group "G", wrote to C.-in-C. West on that day:

"The Army Group does not in the least deny the necessity of weakening the 19th Army to this extent, having regard to the situation of Army Group "B". It nevertheless feels obliged to point out that the consequences of these losses of men and *matériel* will be such that the Army's defences will be so diminished that it cannot guarantee to hold the coastline."

On August 10, however, the 19th Army had to lose its 338th Division. 11th Panzer Division was ordered to Avignon from Montauban by Hitler, but not until August 13, so that by the following day the whole of this division was still over on the right bank of the Rhône. This was the situation facing General Wiese, C.-in-C. 19th Army.

The German naval forces in the south of France consisted of only a limited number of small units and a few U-boats. The American air forces increased their attacks on Toulon, however, and four U-boats were sunk on August 6. The Luftwaffe had only 70 fighters and 130 bombers, a total of only one-tenth of the Allied aircraft used in Operation "Dragoon".

The first landings

On the single day of August 15, Allied aircraft flew 4,250 sorties and only 60 German planes managed to get off the ground. Admiral Hewitt's fleet fired 50,000 shells, including 3,000 12-inch or heavier, either during the preparations or at the request of the troops landing. The American VI Corps' attack, supported by the "Sudre" Combat Command of the French 1st Armoured Division, was against the German 148th Division (Lieutenant-General Otto Fretter-Pico) on the right and the 242nd Division (Lieutenant-

continued on page 1921

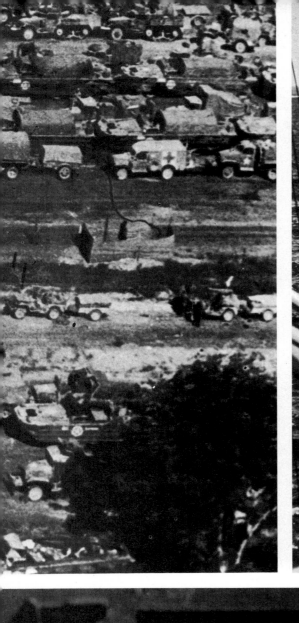

△ *The first paratroops are dropped. The main paratroop force was carried by 396 aircraft in nine relays, and was preceded by pathfinders.*
▷ *One of the glider landing zones. Much had been learned from earlier fiascos, and the German anti-glider defences gave little trouble.*

1916

△ *A spectacular sight—the sky of southern France fills with parachutes. The "Dragoon" operations saw the most successful mass drop to date, with 60 per cent of the paratroops landing on their dropping zones or nearby.*

△ *Familiar scenes on the beaches – order emerges from apparent chaos.*
▷ *Homage to a colossus – a G.I. surveys the deck of one of the two French battle-cruisers in Toulon. (Strasbourg and Dunkerque had both been scuttled at Toulon when the Germans occupied southern France in November 1942.)*
▷▷ *A party of Germans surrenders in Marseilles under a hastily-improvised flag of truce.*

1918

△ *Out in the open at last—the F.F.I. joins up with the liberators.*
▷ *F.F.I. round-up of suspected collaborators in Marseilles.*

continued from page 1914

General Bässler) on the left, the latter being responsible for the defence of Toulon. Both German units were part of LXII Corps (General Neuling) but corps H.Q. at Draguignan was cut off from its troops by the landing of the "Frederick" Division, supported by the Var *maquis.* The only Allied unit to run into difficulties was the U.S. 36th Division (Major-General John E. Dahlquist) in the area of Agay. Everywhere else the operation went like clockwork. By evening the Allies had landed 60,000 men, 6,000 vehicles, and 50,000 tons of *matériel,* all at the cost of 320 killed who, for the most part, had tumbled onto mines.

Amongst the day's exploits those of Colonel Bouvet's commando are worth recording. It landed in the middle of the night between Cavalaire and Cavalière and captured the fortifications on Cap Nègre. By the evening of the 15th it had advanced over nine miles and taken 1,000 prisoners.

Twenty-four hours later the 7th Army beach-head extended from Anthéor on the right through Draguignan, where General Neuling and his staff were taken prisoner, to le Luc on the road to Aix and over 24 miles from Fréjus, then back to the Mediterranean between Cavalière and le Lavandou. On the beaches Patch's second echelon arrived ahead of time and landed with the 1st Moroccan (General Brosset), the 3rd Algerian (General de Monsabert), and the 9th Colonial (General Magnan) Divisions, the remainder of the French 1st Armoured Division (General Touzet du Vigier) and General Guillaume's Moroccan *goumiers,* North African mountain troops.

De Lattre

On the following day this vanguard of the French 1st Army went into battle under General de Lattre de Tassigny. In the exercise of his command de Lattre seemed to be everywhere and to appear as if by miracle in places where his decision was needed. He cared deeply for the fate of his men and was often rude to staff and services on their behalf if the occasion warranted it.

Two men from very different backgrounds have borne witness to his character. On September 30, 1935, as he left manoeuvres at Mailly, Captain Hans Speidel, assistant military attaché at

the German Embassy in Paris, made the following comment on the officer commanding the 151st Regiment: "De Lattre makes an exceptional impression: he is a man of great vitality and fine intelligence and his bearing and discernment are quite out of the ordinary. His fellow-officers predict a great future for him in the French Army." This judgement by Rommel's future chief-of-staff is echoed by General de Gaulle in his memoirs:

"De Lattre was emotional, flexible, far-sighted and a man of wide interests, influencing the minds around him by the ardour of his personality, heading towards his goal by sudden and unexpected leaps, although often well thought out ones.

"De Lattre, on each occasion, courted opportunity above all. Until he found it he endured the ordeal of his tentative efforts, devoured by an impatience that often provoked scenes among his contacts. Suddenly seeing where, when and

▽ *From the beaches of Provence to the Vosges. When the "Dragoon" force joined hands with the right-wing armies advancing from Normandy, the Allied front was extended from the Channel to the Swiss frontier.*
Overleaf: *Another testament to Allied air power – bombed bridges across the Rhône.*

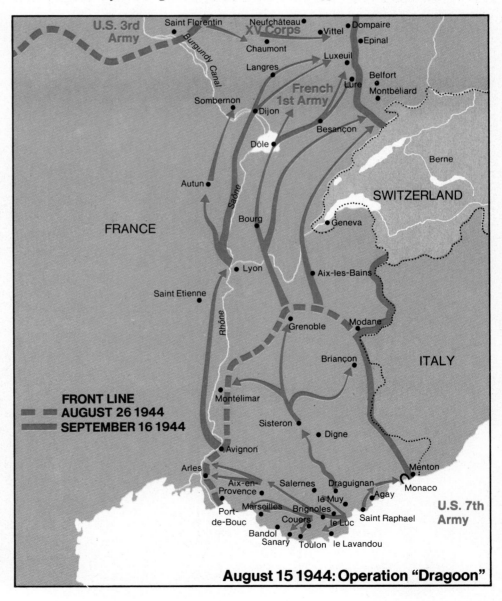

August 15 1944: Operation "Dragoon"

FRONT LINE
AUGUST 26 1944
SEPTEMBER 16 1944

▷ *A group pose by exultant F.F.I. fighters.*
▽ *New weapons for the F.F.I., courtesy of the Allies.*

△ *F.F.I. men shift a wrecked*
vehicle while the Shermans
roll past in the background.
◁ *A wealth of new equipment.*

1925

△ *Keeping up the pressure: a Sherman pushes north. Despite the pace of their advance the French and Americans failed to cut off and annihilate the Germans in the south.*

how the issue could be determined, he then set about the task of building it up and exploiting it. All the resources of a rich personality and extraordinary energy were put to work, demanding a limitless effort of those he engaged in it, but certain that he was preparing them for success.''

It is no disrespect to this strategist and leader of men to say that the weapon Weygand and Giraud had forged for him, and which General Juin had tempered in the recent Italian campaign, had a keen edge. The Frenchmen from North Africa were enthusiastic at the idea that they were going to liberate their brothers in the home country, and were encouraged by the presence amongst them of 18,000 escapees from the unhappy armistice army. Considering the 9th Colonial Division's attack on the German positions in the area of Villars-les-Blamont on November 14 and 22, when the division's artillery crushed the 198th Division in the area of le Puix-Suarce, we can say with some justice that the 1st Army, by its bravery and its accomplishments, was the equal of any other Allied force.

A better judge was Major-General von Mellenthin, then chief-of-staff of Army Group ''G''. In *Panzer Battles* he writes: ''The French tanks, reflecting the tempera-

ment of their army commander, Gener de Lattre de Tassigny, attacked wi extraordinary spirit and *élan*.'' A wortl tribute from an enemy who knew wh he was talking about, to General Vigier and his colleague Vernejou commander of the French 5th Armour Division. The French opened their sco with the capture of Salernes, Brignol and Cuers, the latter some nine mil north-east of Toulon.

The American VI Corps, acting on loc information, sent a motorised colum along the axis Digne–Sisteron with orde to intercept the German 19th Army Montélimar. Close on its heels was t 36th Division. The 45th Division (Majo General William W. Eagles) had tak the road to Aix-en-Provence.

Hitler orders retreat

In view of the reports he had receive and realising that there was no long any hope of throwing the enemy ba into the sea, on August 16 Hitler order Colonel-General Blaskowitz to begin once the evacuation of south and sout west France. Army Group ''G'' wou

Abandoned transport in the wake of the German retreat. Unlike the advancing Allies, Blaskowitz had the advantage of being able to fall back on well-stocked depots as he pulled back up the Rhône valley.

1927

△ Arrival at the Swiss frontier.
▷ American Intelligence men get to work on an impressive haul of captured German maps. The German habit of marking in dispositions directly onto their maps, instead of onto a transparent overlay sheet, was a constant help to Allied Intelligence in dispersing the "fog of war".

link up in the region of Sens with Model's left as the latter fell back to the Seine, whilst the 19th Army would proceed up the Rhône valley and hold as long as possible the line Côte d'Or–Lyon–Aix-les-Bains so as to keep Switzerland encircled. The 242nd Division at Toulon and the 244th at Marseilles (Major-General Schaeffer) would defend the ports to the last and raze their installations to the ground. The 148th Division, fighting in the Estérel massif, and the 157th in the Dauphiné, would come under Field-Marshal Kesselring's command and hold the French side of the Alps.

General von der Chevallerie, C.-in-C. of the German 1st Army, had transferred his H.Q. from Bordeaux to Fontainebleau on August 10 and so the conduct of the German retreat in the south-west fell to General Sachs, commander of LXIV Corps (158th and 159th Divisions). He left strong garrisons in the "fortresses" of la Pointe-de-Grave, Royan, and la Rochelle. General Wiese's task was to co-ordinate the movements of the Luftwaffe IV Corps (General Petersen: 189th, 198th, and 716th Divisions) and LXXXV Corps (338th Division). The 11th Panzer Division, under a particularly distin-

guished commander, Lieutenant-General Gustav von Wietersheim, was ordered to cover the retreat.

Hitler's new directive

On August 20, as a consequence of this order to Army Group "G" and the increasingly serious situation of Army Group "B", whose left flank was being rolled up by Patton and the American 3rd Army, the Führer issued a new directive. This has been summarised by Professor Percy Ernst Schramm, then editor and now publisher of the O.K.W. war diaries for 1944 and 1945:

"C.-in-C. West was ordered to hold the bridgehead west of Paris and prevent the enemy drive towards Dijon. First of all what remained of the 5th *Panzerarmee* and the 7th Army had to be withdrawn behind the River Touques and reorganised so that their armoured formations could be brought back into the left flank. If it turned out to be impossible to hold out in front of the Seine, the Paris bridgehead had to be held and also the line Seine–Yonne – Burgundy Canal – Dijon – Dôle –

Swiss frontier. The withdrawal of the 7th Army behind the Seine was to be prepared at once. The 5th *Panzerarmee* would protect its crossing over to the right bank so as to prevent the enemy engaged in the Seine valley from driving north and then eastwards after crossing the river."

Downstream from Paris the 1st Army, now under Army Group "B", would block off the narrow valleys on either side of Montargis to allow the occupation of the Burgundy Canal and the area north-west of Dijon.

300,000 Germans cut off

This directive calls for two remarks. Firstly, it took no account of the 230,000 men from the army (86,337), navy and air force trapped in the "fortresses" in the West.

Amongst these, Saint Malo had fallen on August 17 after epic resistance. It

took the 8-inch and 240-mm howitzers of the U.S. artillery, the 15-inch guns of the battleship *Warspite,* and the use of napalm to force Colonel von Aulock to hoist the white flag on the little island of Cézembre, the last centre of resistance, on September 2. The Brest garrison was attacked by the U.S. 2nd, 8th, and 29th Divisions and defended with equal tenacity by Lieutenant-General Ramcke and the 2nd Parachute Division. On September 17 fighting ceased in this unhappy town, which had been very heavily shelled. A further 48 hours were to elapse before Ramcke gave up the struggle in the Crozon peninsula.

Neither of the "fortresses" of Lorient or Saint Nazaire on opposite banks of the Loire was attacked; nor were the Channel Islands, where the 319th Division (Lieutenant-General von Schmettow) had some 30,000 men. The latter were sufficiently aware of the futility of their mission to call themselves the "Guernsey P.O.W.s" or the "non-stop card-players". It may be wondered if

the abandonment of some 300,000 men in the pockets of the Channel, the Atlantic, and the Mediterranean was a judicious investment on Hitler's part.

German divisions bled white

Our second remark is that this directive certainly came too late. It might have been possible to carry it out on August 1, when the vanguard of the 4th Panzer Division was forcing a crossing of the Sélune at Pontaubault. But it was no longer possible on the 20th, when Patton was driving his XII and XX Corps towards Sens and Montereau and ordering XV Corps to cross the Seine at Mantes without a moment's delay.

Hitler's directive, overtaken by events, was also at fault because it was issued without regard to the means left at Field-Marshal Model's disposal. In effect,

◁ ◁ △ *Battle-stained G.I.s throng a field kitchen.*
◁ ◁ *The new occupants take over – Americans at work in a former German headquarters.*
△ *A Skink anti-aircraft tank keeps watch at a river crossing. The Skink was a Ram tank fitted with four 20-mm cannon in a special cast turret.*

△ By the end of 1944 the southernmost extremity of the Maginot Line had been reached.

according to H. M. Cole of the historical service of the U.S. Army, who bases his figures on minute research of German military archives, on August 31 the 60-odd divisions of the Wehrmacht and the *Waffen*-S.S. then engaged on the Western Front had lost 293,802 officers, N.C.O.s, and men killed, wounded, and missing since June 6. This was an average of about 5,000 men per division, a loss which must have sapped the strength of every formation. In July the Inspector General of the *Panzerwaffe* recorded the destruction of 282 Pzkw IV, 375 Panther, and 140 Tiger tanks; in August these figures were respectively 279, 358, and 97, giving an overall total of 1,529 in 62 days of fighting. It was the same for the rest of the equipment: by August 25, 1,500 guns, (field, A.A., and anti-tank) and 500 assault guns had been destroyed. The Führer's order to the C.-in-C. West might have been impossible to carry out, but there was also little chance of the latter's beaten armies establishing themselves in the position just reconnoitred by General Kitzinger of the Luftwaffe behind the Seine and the Burgundy Canal. This line ran along the Somme, the Crozat Canal, the Aisne at Soissons, the Marne from Epernay to Chaumont, the Langres plateau, and ended up at the Swiss frontier in the region of Pontarlier.

A new defence line

On August 24 Hitler dictated to Seyss Inquart, the Nazi High Commissioner in Holland, *Gauleiters* Simon, Bürkel, and Wagner (his representatives in Luxembourg, Lorraine, and Alsace), and th military authorities concerned an orde to develop a "German position in th West" for which they would have re course to a mass levy.

There would be a continuous anti tank obstacle, behind which the lan would be laid waste and positions in dept organised. It would straddle the Scheld estuary, use the line of the Albert Canal cover Aix-la-Chapelle and Trier, th fortified complex of Thionville–Metz turn up the Moselle as far as Sain Maurice and finally block the gap a Belfort.

Did Hitler realise that, from Model' reports, his directive of August 20 wa out of date by the 24th? The fact remain that twice in four days he had recognise that he was beaten in the West. As we ca see, respecting Churchill's anguish ove the Franco-American landing in Pro vence, Operation "Dragoon" took no 90 days but 48 hours to assist Genera Eisenhower's offensive.

CHAPTER 130
"Paris Liberée!"

On August 16, the very day when the American XX Corps reached Chartres, the Paris police went on strike. This was the start of the uprising in the city. S.H.A.E.F.'s plan was not to mount a frontal attack on an urban area of this importance, but to outflank it on both sides so that it would fall of its own accord, thus sparing the city the fighting and all the destruction this would entail. According to calculations made in London, this operation was to take place between 120 and 150 days after D-Day. On August 16 at Chartres General Patton was about 20 days ahead of schedule.

"What to do about Paris?" Eisenhower asked himself. A critical problem indeed, as he has pointed out in his memoirs, since the liberation of Paris would bring the need for supplying food to the capital at a rate calculated by S.H.A.E.F. experts at 4,000 tons a day. This figure caused the C.-in-C. 12th Army Group to say "no":

"However, in spite of this danger of famine in Paris, I was determined that we would not be dissuaded from our plan to by-pass the city. If we could rush on to the Siegfried Line with tonnage that might otherwise be diverted to Paris, the city would be compensated for its additional week of occupation with an earlier end to the war. But we had not reckoned with the impatience of those Parisians who had waited four years for the armies that now approached their gates. My plan to pinch out Paris was exploded on an airstrip near Laval the morning of August 23."

General de Gaulle, in his rôle of head of the provisional government, had also addressed himself to the Allied C.-in-C. On August 21, newly arrived at Rennes

▽ *The ecstasy of liberation. A convoy of civilian cars follows Allied vehicles in a spontaneous demonstration during the liberation of Paris. It was some days before the city was completely free of snipers, though the bulk of German forces had surrendered by August 25.*

△ *Shooting continued after the surrender. Here members of the "F.F.I." return fire during General de Gaulle's visit to Notre-Dame. Note the insignia painted on the police cars, the "Lorraine Cross" of de Gaulle's Free French (partly visible on the door of the left-hand car), and the initials of the underground army that captured Paris (on the bonnet of the car at the right).*

from Algiers, he had said:

"Information reaching me from Paris leads me to believe that as the police and the German armed forces have almost disappeared from the city, and as there is an extreme shortage of food, serious trouble may be expected within a very short time. I think it is vital to occupy Paris as soon as possible with French and Allied troops, even if some fighting results and there is some damage in the city.

"If a disorderly situation arises now in Paris, it will be difficult later on to get control of the city without serious incidents and this could even affect later operations.

"I am sending you General Koenig, who has been nominated Military Governor of Paris and C.-in-C. of the Paris Region, to study the occupation question with you in case, as I request of you, you decide to proceed without delay."

In his war memoirs de Gaulle tells us

why he intervened. It was a matter of preventing the formation, under cover of an uprising, of a predominantly Communist government. If this were to happen, he said, "on my arrival I should find this 'popular' government functioning: it would crown me with a laurel wreath, invite me to take my place within its organisation, and then pull all the strings. For those in control the rest would then be alternate boldness and prudence, the spread of state interference everywhere under cover of purges, suppression of public opinion by control of information and a militia, the progressive elimination of their earlier associates until the dictatorship of the proletariat was established."

Eisenhower agreed to the request, and Leclerc's division was sent off to Paris. This was what they had been waiting for, stamping with impatience until they were given free rein, ever since they had been transferred from North Africa to Grea

the Soviet advance would sooner or later burst over the dykes the Germans were erecting to hold it, and flood out all over Germany. Events since 1943 had only served to confirm his pessimism. When he left the O.K.W. meeting on August 7 after being invested by Hitler with the command of *Gross Paris* he had the impression that he had been dealing with a madman:

"Finally Hitler came to July 20 and I witnessed the explosion of a man filled to bursting with hatred. He yelled at me that he was glad to have bagged the whole opposition at one go and that he would crush it. He was in a state of feverish excitement. Saliva was literally running from his mouth. He was trembling all over and the desk on which he was leaning shook with him. He was bathed in perspiration and became more agitated still as he shouted that his generals would be 'strung up'. I was convinced there and then: the man opposite me was mad!"

If the means at Choltitz's disposal were enough to contain an uprising within the capital, the situation became completely different on August 21 as soon as O.K.W. ordered that the "Paris bridgehead" was to be held against the Americans. One could no doubt, as did the Führer, stress the "supreme importance of the defence of Paris from the military and political points of view" and declare that "its fall would cause the breakdown of the whole coastal front north of the Seine and compel us to abandon bases used by

△ *A German officer, pistol in hand, races past a Parisian café. He was photographed from one of the commanding positions held by the F.F.I. just before he was shot. The Germans fought at a disadvantage in Paris since they did not dominate the rooftops, which in turn meant that they could not control the streets. As in Warsaw they retreated to the major buildings, which they held as strongpoints.*

▽ *Two soldiers of the U.S. 4th Infantry Division shelter behind a truck as they watch for snipers.*

ritain. Meanwhile this French 2nd Armoured Division had been moved from he U.S. 3rd to the U.S. 1st Army and ut under V Corps. The least that can be aid about this new arrangement is that enerals Gerow and Leclerc just were ot on the same wavelength.

Choltitz and Hitler

n the German side the principal actors n the drama where General Dietrich von Choltitz, the Swedish Consul-General aoul Nordling, and the leaders of the aris insurrection.

Choltitz's behaviour is to be explained hus: since the previous autumn, hen he had commanded XLVIII Panzer orps on the Dniepr, he had maintained, n the presence of his chief-of-staff, Major-eneral von Mellenthin, that the tide of

18 au 25 Août 1944

Colonel Roll-Tanguy

Colonel Fabien

PARIS *SE LIBÈRE*

our V-weapons against England". And Choltitz could also be reminded that "ir the course of history the loss of Paris has also meant the loss of France". This dic not, however, alter in any way the situa tion of the 22,000 men from two or three different divisions with whom he was being asked to hold a bridgehead from the Seine at Poissy to the Marne at Cretei (about 32 miles). The end of the order "The Seine bridges will be prepared for destruction. Paris must only fall into enemy hands as a heap of rubble", re vealed more a state of terrorism than sound strategic thinking. As an experienced soldier Choltitz was well aware tha neither the heap of rubble nor the des truction of the bridges (if they were al blown) would slow down the Allied advance. There would have to be more than 60 demolition charges laid, two o three at least would fail to go off and al the experience of the Blitzkrieg had shown that destroyed bridges are no good unless protected by covering fire. For al these reasons the C.-in-C. *Gross Pari* lent a willing ear to Raoul Nordling, no however forgetting that in German the freedom and perhaps the lives o his wife and children might depend o the way his behaviour was judged by th Führer. In this double life he was com pelled to live he was ably seconded b Lieutenant-General Speidel, chief-of staff of Army Group "B", though the both had to converse in guarded term because their telephones were liable t be tapped.

Paris liberated

On August 23 the French 2nd Armoured Division bore down on Paris, the "Lang lade" and "Dio" Combat Command along the axis Sées–Rambouillet– de Sèvres, and the "Billotte" Comba Command via Alençon–Chartres–Arpa jon–Porte d'Italie, causing an overla along the sector given by U.S. V Corp to its 4th Division and a new disagreemer between Generals Gerow and Leclerc During the advance German 8.8-cm gun in ambush along the roads caused the los of 317 men and 41 tanks and self-propelle guns. In the night of August 24-25 Captai Dronne and the tanks *Romilly, Champan bert,* and *Montmirail* passed throug the Porte de Gentilly and reached th square in front of the Hôtel de Ville.

1936

△ A group of German soldiers emerges from a building to surrender to the F.F.I.
◁ A German officer stands perilously outside the Chamber of Deputies, during the negotiations for the surrender of the 400 Germans who had held out inside.
◁ ◁ A children's magazine with a rather imaginative picture of the liberation.
▽ ◁ General Koenig and staff. Cdt. Duperior, Col. de Chevigné, Capt. Lucas, Koenig, Col. de Wavrin, Comm. Raulin.

▽ A Renault R40 returned to its original owners: members of the "F.F.I." refuel a tank captured from the Germans.

1937

Summer in Paris. Crowds near the Opera ignore a burning vehicle as they surge into the square to celebrate the liberation. The battle for Paris was a curious blend of street fighting and the continued life of a city. Hitler had hoped to reduce the city to ruins with air and artillery attacks complementing the planned demolitions.

On the following day, with the aid of the *Forces Françaises de l'Intérieur* under Colonel Rol-Tanguy, the 2nd Armoured Division liberated Paris, and Choltitz, who had not left his headquarters in the Hôtel Meurice, surrendered.

"Destroy Paris!"

As soon as he heard that Paris had fallen, Hitler flew into a rage and ordered it to be wiped out. With this end in view he had the great siege mortar *Karl* readied. This huge gun had a calibre of 60 cms (23.6 inches), fired 2.2-ton shells, and had not been in action since Sevastopol'. The V-weapons and all available aircraft were now also to be brought into action.

Speidel forbade the transmission of this order. It had not the least strategic value and it would have caused thousands of civilian victims, and the destruction of buildings of inestimable artistic value. Speidel was therefore not only relieved of his post but arrested, imprisoned, and only spared by a miracle from the horrible torture which befell Witzleben and Hoeppner. If any conclusion is to be drawn from this episode it must come in the form of a question: what stage would the intellectual and moral reconstruction of Western Europe have reached today if Generals von Choltitz and Speidel had not, at the risk of their lives, thwarted the bloodthirsty plans of Adolf Hitler?

De Lattre presses on . . .

In Provence, General de Lattre de Tassigny had meanwhile managed to wriggle out of the plan by which he was intended to concentrate all his efforts on Toulon, and only move on to Marseilles when the large military port had been mopped up. This plan was calculated to lead to the hoisting of the tricolour on Notre Dame de la Garde on D-day plus 45, that is on September 28, if all went well.

On August 18 two solutions seemed possible to this ardent, yet calculating leader, as he says in his memoirs: "Given our recent successes, ought I to stick to the original plan? Or should I try to extend its scope? These were the alternatives that faced me on that day. It was very difficult, for the consequences of an error of judgement could only be very serious. If I opted for prudence, I could attack in strength, but all the benefits of surprise, and the chaos this would have caused in the enemy's ranks, would be lost. The Germans would have time to redeploy, move up reserves, and make full use of the enormous capabilities of the Toulon defence system. Thus caution would mean a siege, with all its consequent delays and suffering.

"If, on the other hand, I opted for boldness, I could expect to profit from the confusion caused by the strength of Truscott's attack, but my men would have to attack with one man against two, in the open and against reinforced concrete and protected gun emplacements. Boldness could break the French Army before it was even brought together.

"These were dramatic moments for the soul of a commander, but they could not be prolonged. After all, if the surprise attack failed, I could halt it and allow another commander to try again with more reinforcements. The risk was small compared with the enormous gains that might result from a swift success."

De Lattre went for boldness and got the

Two scenes typical of the liberation.
△ *A Parisienne gives a G.I. a victor's greeting, watched by a smiling gendarme.*

▽ *Police and members of the "F.F.I." escort away a suspected collaborator. The round-up of suspects after the liberation was haphazard and at times unjust.*

approval of General Patch, who overcame the misgivings of his staff. The French commander was, we would suggest, bolstering up a right decision with wrong premises, because on the same day, far from thinking of reinforcing the defence of Marseilles and Toulon, his adversary, acting under a directive from O.K.W., was actually putting into effect an order for withdrawal which was to take his 19th Army back to the area Lyons–Aix-les-Bains. De Lattre did not know, and could not have known, that Wiese was getting ready to retreat. The risk he mentioned was a real one to him and had to be faced.

This points to the difference between the military historian and the war-time commander: the one draws upon documents calmly collated in the peace of a library; the other makes his decisions from information which is never complete and "works on human skin", as Catherine the Great remarked forcibly to the intellectual Diderot, who carried no responsibility.

Now left to its fate, 242nd Division defended Toulon to the last ounce of its

△ *Sheltering behind an American tank, civilians shoot at a building still held by German troops.*
◁ *Parisians take cover behind parked M7 "Priest" self-propelled guns, during a battle with a sniper. These fire fights were often one-sided, for no snipers were ever captured, and Frenchmen found on the roof tops claimed that they too were hunting Milice gunmen or German stragglers. (The Milice was the hated Vichy militia).*

strength. On August 21 the 1st Free French Division had got as far as Hyères, in spite of stiff resistance, and Colonel Bouvet's commandos, working under the 9th Colonial Division, had scaled the walls of Fort Coudon on ropes and hunted down the 120 men of the garrison in the galleries: "At 1530 hours," General de Lattre reported, "when the Kriegsmarine decided to give in, it had only six unwounded men. But at the moment of surrender, their commander signalled: 'Fire on us.' Violent shelling then began on the fort and lasted for several minutes. Germans and Frenchmen alike were hit, and amongst the latter was Lieutenant Girardon, one of the heroes of the assault."

Defended to the last man

The same thing happened the next day in the ammunition magazine at Toulon, where the galleries had to be taken one by one by Lieutenant-Colonel Gambiez's battalion of shock troops, supported by two tank-destroyers firing point-blank and a battalion of artillery, which reduced the works above the ground.

"Only the dead stopped fighting," de Lattre wrote when describing this action. At nightfall, when the flame-throwers had overcome the last of the resistance, he went on, "the inside of the fortress is nothing more than a huge open charnel-

house over which hangs a frightful stench of death. It is being devoured by flames which cause boxes of ammunition to explode at every moment. There are 250 corpses strewn on the ground and only 180 men have been taken prisoner. Of these 60 are seriously wounded. This macabre spectacle suddenly reminded me of the most tragic sights at Douaumont and Thiaumont in 1916. It is a fine thing that our lads, many of whom are in battle for the first time, have equalled the exploits of the hardened *poilus* of Verdun. Their enemy was in no way inferior to the one their fathers faced. One of the defenders was asked to give the reason for this heroic and desperate resistance. 'We defended ourselves, that's all. I am an officer, a lieutenant. It's war for me as well as for you, gentlemen,' he replied."

The victorious advance of the 9th Colonial Division through the defences of Toulon relieved the 3rd Algerian Division of its first mission, during which

◁ *Behind his own barricade, a French soldier covers a road with a .50 calibre machine gun.*
▽ ◁ *An M8 light armoured car of the 4th U.S. Infantry Division drives down the Champs Elysées. Four years earlier the soldiers and horses of the Wehrmacht had clattered down the same wide avenues.*
▽ *Two German officers and a medical orderly are escorted away by a mixed group of "F.F.I." and regular French soldiers. With the large numbers of small arms in circulation in August 1944, these Germans were still targets for revenge by individual Frenchmen even when they had become prisoners.*

1943

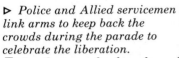 Police and Allied servicemen link arms to keep back the crowds during the parade to celebrate the liberation.
▽ Another parade of trucks and soldiers, a painting by Floyd Davis "German prisoners in Paris". A 2½-ton truck with its human cargo drives past Notre-Dame in the bleak autumn months following the liberation.

1944

it had reached Sanary and Bandol, thus ensuring the investment of the western side of the fortress.

Reinforced in due time by General Guillaume's *goums*, General de Monsabert rapidly turned towards Marseilles, where the firemen, the sailors, and the F.F.I. had taken up arms on August 21. The French forces took the mountain route and outflanked 244th Division's defence points along the main axes. On the 23rd General de Monsabert presented himself at 15th Military District H.Q. He sent for Lieutenant-General Schäffer, who then refused to surrender.

Toulon liberated

The liberation of Toulon was completed on August 27 by the capitulation of Rear-Admiral Ruhfus, who had found a last refuge from the shells of the navy and the bombs of the air force in the Saint Mandrier peninsula. The assault on Toulon had cost the French 2,700 men killed and wounded, but they had taken over 17,000 prisoners and several hundred guns. The Cape Cépet battery, which had been such a thorn in the flesh of the attackers, was pounded by 1,400 shells of 12-inch calibre or higher and 809 1,000- and 2,000-lb bombs. There were four direct hits on its turrets. One jammed, the other had one gun put out of action. The only gun undamaged fired 250 shells, but without appreciable effect.

Marseilles falls

On August 23 de Lattre sent the 1st Armoured Division into Marseilles, and together with the 3rd Algerian Division and the Moroccan *goums* it overcame the resistance within the city. As in Toulon, the Germans defended themselves bitterly, using rocket launchers, mines, and flame-throwers. The loss successively of Notre Dame de la Garde and Fort Saint Nicolas, however, ended Schäffer's resistance and in the evening of the 27th he wrote to Monsabert:

"Prolonged resistance seems pointless in view of your superior strength. I ask you to cease firing from 2100 to 0800 hours so that surrender terms may be finalised for mid-day on the 28th and that I may have a decision from you which will

allow me either to surrender with honour or to fight to the finish."

Neither General de Monsabert nor his commander were men to overlook the valour of the 244th Division. And so the armistice was signed on August 28 shortly before 0800 hours.

Allied victory in Provence

The Allies were now a month ahead of schedule. The fury of their attacks had cost them 4,000 killed and wounded, but they had wiped out two enemy divisions and captured 37,000 prisoners.

Before ceasing all resistance the Germans blew up the port installations in Marseilles and Toulon. Until these were restored, the Provence beaches had landed 380,000 men, 69,312 vehicles, 306,000 tons of supplies and *matériel,* and 17,848 tons of fuel. By May 8, 1945, 905,512 men and 4,123,794 tons of *matériel* had passed through the hastily-reconstructed ports of Marseilles, Toulon, and Port de Bouc. These figures are taken from Morison, who claims, and we would agree with him, that for this alone Operation "Dragoon" was justified.

△ *General Dwight D. Eisenhower, Supreme Commander Allied Expeditionary Forces, at the Arc de Triomphe, when he visited Paris on September 1, 1944. With him are* (left) *Lieutenant-General Omar N. Bradley and* (right) *General Joseph Koenig, military commander of Paris, and Air Chief-Marshal Arthur Tedder* (extreme right). *Koenig, the hero of Bir Hakeim, was to comment a few days after the liberation "The worst danger in Paris at the moment are the F.F.I."*

▷ Light tanks of the Fighting French drive down the Champs Elysées in a victory parade shared by citizens and soldiers.
▷ A French colour party in an American Dodge command car. The soldiers are from the French North African Army, which served in Italy, France, and Germany. The Germans were to pay tribute to its fighting spirit and the quality of the leadership, which came as a bitter surprise after the easy victories of 1940. Like the British Indian Army it attracted men dedicated to soldiering, for even in the peace-time years before the war, there were skirmishes and fire fights with warring tribes.
◁ Smiling for the camera. Part of the crowds that turned out to greet the American forces entering Paris.

CHAPTER 131
Across the Seine

In late August 1944 the Franco-American victory in Provence thus usefully complemented the Anglo-American victory in Normandy. All those who followed the progress of the war on wall maps and every day moved the little blue flags representing the Allied forces further north, north-east, and east, must have thought that on the Western Front the Germans were on the point of final collapse and the Third Reich on the eve of invasion. On August 26, the 21st Army Group had the left of its Canadian 1st Army in the area of Honfleur and linked up with the British 2nd Army around Louviers; the right of the British 2nd Army was in Vernon, where it had a bridgehead on the north bank of the Seine. Between Mantes and Saint Nazaire,

the American 12th Army Group formed an immense hairpin including the Seine crossings at Mantes, Paris, Melun, and Troyes, then through Saint Florentin and Joigny, back to the Loire at Gien. In the south, whilst the 7th Army Group (U.S. 7th and French 1st Armies) was mopping up in Toulon and Marseilles, the American VI Corps had liberated Grenoble and was trying to cut off the retreat of the German 19th Army in the area of Montélimar.

By September 10 the Germans had only three fortresses in the north of France: Boulogne, Calais, and Dunkirk. Montgomery, newly appointed a Field-Marshal, occupied Bruges, Ghent, and Antwerp whilst his 2nd Army, down river from Hasselt, was on the north bank of

▽ *An M10 tank destroyer crosses a pontoon bridge over the Seine on August 24, 1944. On the far bank three cranes, used in the assembly of the pneumatic pontoons and bridging bays, bear witness to the wealth of equipment available to the U.S. forces in Europe.*

the Albert Canal. The American 12th Army Group was in Liège, Bastogne, and Luxembourg, and on the outskirts of Thionville, Metz, and Nancy. Until its XV Corps came back into the line, the 3rd Army had its right flank exposed in the area of Neufchâteau, but by September 11 it was in contact at Sambernon with the French II Corps, which formed the left wing of the Franco-American 7th Army Group. The right flank of this army group was in Pont-de-Roide near the Swiss border. Finally, between Mont Blanc and the Mediterranean Kesselring still held on to Modane and Briançon for a few days, but Savoy, the Dauphiné, Provence, and the Alpes Maritimes were virtually free.

This exceptionally rapid progress and the capture of 402,000 prisoners reported in the Allied communiqué of September 15 caused wild optimism at S.H.A.E.F. and at the headquarters of the 21st and 12th Army Groups. Between June 6 and September 11, German losses in killed and wounded were no greater than 40,000 and 20,000 respectively. Eisenhower now had 49 divisions in the field.

It is not surprising that the editor of the information bulletin at S.H.A.E.F. should blow the victory trumpet and write:

"Two and a half months of bitter fighting, culminating for the Germans in a bloodbath big enough even for their extravagant tastes, have brought the end of the war in Europe within sight, almost within reach. The strength of the German Armies in the West has been shattered, Paris belongs to France again, and the Allied armies are streaming towards the frontiers of the Reich." A few days later he concluded:

"The only way the enemy can prevent our advance into Germany will be by reinforcing his retreating forces by divisions from Germany and other fronts and manning the more important sectors of the Siegfried Line with these forces. It is doubtful whether he can do this in time and in sufficient strength."

Montgomery suggests a "concentrated effort" . . .

Montgomery agreed with this forecast and desired S.H.A.E.F. to come to a quick decision about the form and direction to be given to the pursuit. As early as August 17 he had given General Bradley an outline plan of operations which was, in essence:

1. After crossing the Seine, the 12th and 21st Army Groups would form a "solid mass of some forty divisions" which would move north of the Ardennes and put a pincer round the Ruhr, the 12th to the south and the 21st to the

△ *A stone railway bridge blown by the retreating Germans. The charges had been placed in the arches of the bridge, which means that the piers remained intact and could be used as a foundation for a Bailey bridge. Europe suffered severe dislocation to its communications as a result of Allied air attacks and systematic German demolitions.*

△ *An American white phosphorus shell lands in a village in Lorraine. Euphemistically designated a smoke shell, phosphorus was a terrifying anti-personnel weapon, particularly when used against troops in confined conditions.*

north.

2. South of the Ardennes a "strong American force" would be "positioned in the general area Orléans–Troyes–Châlons–Reims–Laon with its right flank thrown back along the R. Loire to Nantes".

3. The American 7th Army Group would be directed from Lyons to Nancy and the Saar. But, Montgomery remarked: "We ourselves must not reach out with our right to join it and thus unbalance our strategy." He concluded: "The basic object of the movement would be to establish a powerful air force in Belgium to secure bridge-heads over the Rhine before the winter began and to seize the Ruhr quickly." According to Montgomery, Bradley

agreed with the plan, whereas in his memoirs the former C.-in-C. 12th Army Group makes no mention of it. It is common knowledge, however, that Eisenhower was unwilling to ratify the suggestions of Montgomery, though the latter returned to the question on August 22 through Major-General Sir de Guingand, his chief-of-staff and, on the following day, in person during talks which took place between the two leaders alone at Condé-sur-Noireau. But, on the point of taking over the conduct of land operations himself, General Eisenhower rejected the idea with his customary affability. In fact, though Montgomery did not expressly say so, the formation of a "solid mass of some forty divisions" to operate north of the Ardennes would ave meant the inclusion of the whole American 1st Army. In a note which he ent to his chief-of-staff on August 22, moreover, he implicitly excluded Bradley rom any part in the race for the Ruhr, ven attempting to dissuade Eisenhower rom his intention of effectively controlling land operations. This can be read etween the lines of paragraphs 3, 4, and of Montgomery's note which de Guinrand handed to Eisenhower:

'3. Single control and direction of the land operations is vital for success. This is a WHOLE TIME JOB for one man.

4. The great victory in N.W. France has been won by personal command. Only in this way will future victories be won. If staff control of operations is allowed to creep in, then quick success becomes endangered.

5. To change the system of command now, after having won a great victory, would be to prolong the war."

Eisenhower was in no way inclined to upport a plan contrary to the agreement f the preceding winter. But neither did e intend to accept the plan which reduced Bradley and his 12th Army Group to some en divisions, invited to mark time on the utskirts of the Argonne—for that is what he "strong American force" would have mounted to. Even if he had fallen in with Montgomery's ideas, he would probably ave been caught between the discontent f Patton, Hodges, and Bradley and the epudiation of his action by the Pentagon.

By preferring to the concentrated effort roposed by Montgomery a wide-front ursuit aimed at both the Ruhr and the aar, did Eisenhower nullify the Anglo-American victory in Normandy? Montgomery's memoirs, finished in September 1958, do suggest this. Events seem to have borne it out, since by December 15 Hodges was bogged down before the Rur and Patton was only just approaching the Saar.

△ *Covered with autumn leaves, U.S. soldiers wait in an abandoned German trench.*

The Eisenhower-Montgomery controversy

It must not be assumed that the "concentrated effort" would have brought the Allies out-and-out victory before the first snows fell. If Patton had been halted on the Troyes – Châlons – Rheims front, Model and Rundstedt would not have lost the forces he trapped and decimated between the Marne and the Moselle, with a loss to the Germans of 22,600 prisoners, 474 tanks, and 482 guns. Also, if the inner flanks of Patton and Patch had not linked up, it would not have been possible to trap the 19,600 Germans whose capture Major-General Elster reported to U.S. 81st Division H.Q. at Beaugency on September 8.

When Montgomery's memoirs appeared, Eisenhower was President of the United States and thus not in a position to answer them. Even after he had left the White House he still remained silent. He would appear to have stuck throughout to his original opinion as expressed in 1949 in *Crusade in Europe* when, denying that the Allies could have overrun the enemy, he concluded: "General Montgomery was acquainted

▽ *A Sherman tank rumbles across a newly-completed pontoon bridge over the Seine at Vulaines-sur-Seine. Construction bridging techniques and light-weight equipment used by the Allies have ended the image of the military engineer as a soldier shoulder deep in a river struggling with timber and rope.*

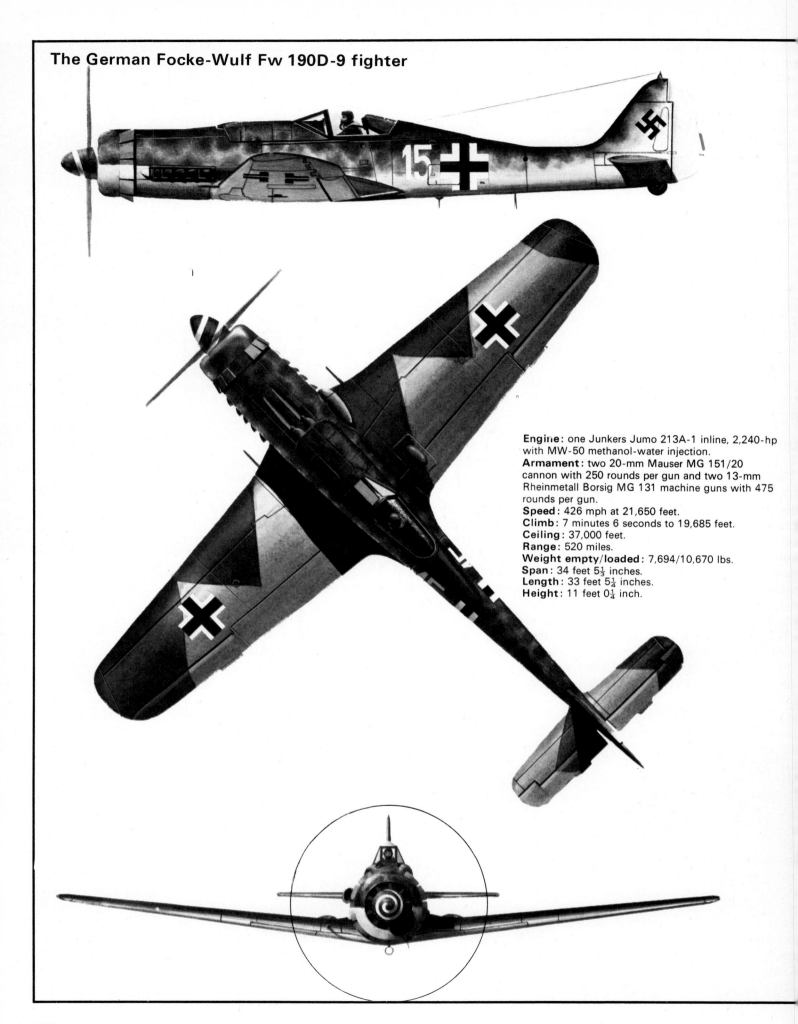

The German Focke-Wulf Fw 190D-9 fighter

Engine: one Junkers Jumo 213A-1 inline, 2,240-hp with MW-50 methanol-water injection.
Armament: two 20-mm Mauser MG 151/20 cannon with 250 rounds per gun and two 13-mm Rheinmetall Borsig MG 131 machine guns with 475 rounds per gun.
Speed: 426 mph at 21,650 feet.
Climb: 7 minutes 6 seconds to 19,685 feet.
Ceiling: 37,000 feet.
Range: 520 miles.
Weight empty/loaded: 7,694/10,670 lbs.
Span: 34 feet $5\frac{1}{3}$ inches.
Length: 33 feet $5\frac{1}{4}$ inches.
Height: 11 feet $0\frac{1}{4}$ inch.

only with the situation in his own sector. He understood that to support his proposal would have meant stopping dead for weeks all units except the Twenty-first Army Group. But he did not understand the impossible situation that would have developed along the rest of our great front when he, having outrun the possibility of maintenance, was forced to stop and withdraw."

A very pertinent remark, we would suggest, as on the right bank of the Rhine, somewhere between Wesel and Munster, it is difficult to imagine what chances of success the 21st Army Group would have had if the 12th had been stuck back at Châlons-sur-Marne through lack of fuel and ammunition. Instead of a "reverse Schlieffen plan" such as Montgomery had envisaged, we might have seen Rundstedt manoeuvring between Montgomery and Bradley as Hindenburg had done 30 years before between Rennenkampf and Samsonov at Tannenberg.

Logistical crisis

The Allies were clearly winning. In spite of their spectacular progress, however, between August 25 and September 10 a number of mishaps and strokes of bad luck, combined with shortages on the logistic side which got worse after the Seine had been crossed, brought Eisenhower to a virtual standstill at the end of September, whereas the Wehrmacht was recovering with astonishing speed.

Was this crisis in supplies the fault of Lieutenant-General J. C. H. Lee, Quartermaster-General at S.H.A.E.F., whom Bradley called "brilliant but niggling"? It was he who controlled the organisation and the running of transport. It must be remembered that Patch in front of Belfort, Patton at Nancy, Hodges at Aix-la-Chapelle, Dempsey on the Albert Canal, and Crerar between Boulogne and Zeebrugge were all being supplied via the beaches of Provence and Normandy. But when the German engineers withdrew, they had carried out 4,000 demolitions over and above the damage caused by Allied bombing in the first six months of the year. The French national railway network was in ribbons and its rolling stock reduced to practically nothing after German requisitioning and Allied air attacks. It is not, therefore, surprising that supplies had not been able to keep

up with the advancing troops, in spite of the so-called "Red Ball Highways", major one-way roads along which the heavy lorries rolled for 20 hours a day. It must also be remembered that Americans, British, Canadians, and French were all several months ahead of schedule. The Allies repaired the ports with astonishing speed, but even so the enemy was still able to re-assemble his scattered forces and prepare for a final thrust.

Certain mishaps also occurred in Allied strategy. The American 7th Army failed in its attempt to cut the retreat of the German 19th Army. The Germans did, it is true, leave 5,000 prisoners, including Lieutenant-General Richter, commander of the 198th Division, at Montélimar, and had only 64 guns left out of the 1,480 of the preceding August 15. But, General de Lattre tells us, Wiese "knew his job" and, moreover, the French and the Americans were always running out of petrol.

On the left the French II Corps (General de Monsabert: 1st Free French Infantry and 1st Armoured Divisions), which crossed the Rhône at Avignon on August 29, liberated Lyons on September 2 and

△ A U.S. 75-mm pack howitzer in action. The mainstay of both the British and U.S. airborne forces, this weapon was also used in the Far East where it was stripped down for animal pack as well as parachute dropping. Possibly the most unusual employment of this versatile weapon was its mounting in U.S. Boston and Mitchell medium bombers in a ground attack and anti-submarine rôle.

1953

△ *The David and Goliath bridges at Vernon on the Seine, built by Sappers of the 43rd (Wessex) Division. The heavy girder bridge in the foreground is being manoeuvred into position by a tug, while a bay (two pontoons attached by panels) can be seen anchored to the assault bridge. With the light assault bridge completed, work on "Goliath" could be started from both banks of the river.*

▷ *Eisenhower begins to batter down Germany's protective gate.*

won a brilliant victory over a detachment of the German 1st Army in the area of Autun on September 9. This gave it Dijon 48 hours later. In the centre the U.S. VI Corps, operating along the axis Bourg en Bresse–Besançon, was held up at Luxeuil and Lure. Finally, on the right was a French group, consisting mainly of the 3rd Algerian Division, the 9th Colonial having had to be stopped when it reached the Swiss frontier between Geneva and Pont-de-Roide. On September 6 General de Lattre formed this group into the French I Corps and put it under the command of General Béthouart. The following day it was held up for lack of ammunition. It held on to its position on top of le Lomont, where the old fort had been captured by the F.F.I at the end of July and from which the Germans had been unable to dislodge them. This was an exploit which, de Lattre says, "gives us an incomparable observation post over the plain of Montbéliard and the 'watchdog' of the Belfort gap. The 3rd Algerian Division is in sight of the promised land, but it is out of breath after its terrific run and can't get in."

We now go over to the American 12th Army Group. The chapter of Patton's war memoirs dealing with this part of the campaign is entitled *Touring with an Army in France*. He could also have adapted the message Colonel-General von Kleist is supposed to have sent to Field-Marshal List in the race for the Caucasus in July 1942: "In front of us, no enemy; behind us, no supplies." On August 25, Patton had been ordered to reach in one bound the line Vitry-le-François–Châlons–Rheims; he was then to move off from there, on the orders of army group, to take the Rhine bridges between Mannheim and Koblenz.

Patton still had under his command U.S. VIII Corps, then occupied in taking Brest. His other units were two corps and six divisions: at Troyes was XII Corps under Major-General Manton S. Eddy, who had just relieved General Cook, evacuated after a heart attack; in the bridgehead at Montereau XX Corps was eager and ready for the chase.

On August 28, XII Corps crossed the Marne at Châlons where 80th Infantry and 4th Armoured Divisions filled up with

petrol thanks to a captured German dump of 88,000 gallons. On the following day XX Corps passed through Epernay and Château-Thierry, then occupied Rheims without any difficulty.

In spite of the threat of petrol supplies running out, Patton had got Bradley's agreement that he should push on from the Marne to the Meuse, and Eddy captured the river crossings at Vaucouleurs, Commercy, and Saint Mihiel on the last day of the month. On his left, Major-General W. H. Walker, after an advance of some 75 miles, occupied Verdun and crossed the river, the bridges being still intact thanks to the F.F.I. But, writes Martin Blumenson, "in possession of Meuse River bridge-heads between Verdun and Commercy, Patton was in position to attack toward the Moselle between Metz and Nancy, and from there the Rhine River was barely a hundred miles away. This was his intention, but by then his supply lines were drawn to the breaking point. Soldiers in the forward echelons needed shoes, heavy underwear, and socks, and these items could not move fast enough to reach the advancing spearheads. The mechanical beasts of burden needed spare parts and maintenance. Still the most critical shortage was gasoline . . . By then the army was virtually bone dry. Individual tanks were dropping out of combat formations for lack of gasoline. The chance of speedy resumption of the pursuit east of the Meuse, a hope that depended on motorised columns, appeared nil."

Eisenhower puts the brake on Patton

Patton tried to get Eisenhower to change his point of view, urging that the way to the Rhine between Mannheim and Koblenz was virtually wide open to his tanks, the Siegfried Line not being strongly held. His eloquence failed to move Eisenhower.

By September 15 the enemy was considerably reinforced and, though Patton had liberated Nancy, he had lost any hope he might have had of breaking the *Westwall* in his stride or even taking Metz

△ *Three Sherman flail tanks cross a Bailey pontoon bridge at Elbeuf on the Seine. The bridge was destroyed by the R.A.F., who also sank the barge seen in the foreground. The use of Bailey bridges kept up the momentum of the Allied advance, and the bridges also helped in the reconstruction of post-war Europe.*

and Thionville on the way. XV Corps, given to him somewhat late in the day, was engaged on his right in the area Chaumont–Neufchâteau. This gave rise to a battle on September 13 between Vittel and Epinal during which the "Langlade" Combat Command of the French 2nd Armoured Division, sharing equally the honours with the 406th Group, U.S. 9th Air Force from Rennes (365 miles away), severely trounced the newly-formed 112th Panzer Brigade, destroying 34 Panther and 26 Pzkw IV tanks out of the 96 it had set out with.

As we have seen, the U.S. 1st Army, with its right in Melun and its left in Mantes, though not entirely under the command of the Anglo-Canadian 21st Army Group, was given the rôle of supporting, along the Aix-la-Chapelle–Cologne axis, Montgomery's drive through the north of the Ruhr. And so, in the matter of fuel and transport, General Hodges was relatively well supplied.

On the right, U.S. VII Corps with it 3rd Armoured Division (Major-Genera Maurice Rose) in the lead, broke out the Melun bridgehead, passed throug Laon on August 30, and crossed the France Belgian frontier from Avesnes and Mau beuge, getting into Mons at dusk o September 2.

On the left of the U.S. 1st Army, XI Corps advanced at the same speed alon the axis Mantes–Montdidier–Cambrai Tournai. 25,000 Germans from 20 differer divisions were trapped between the tw advancing American columns betwee Mons and Cambrai and surrendered t VII Corps by order of General Straub commanding LXXIV Corps.

From Mons and Tournai VII and XI Corps then changed direction from nort to north-east, the former towards Lièg which it reached on September 8, the latte towards the Albert Canal, where it mad contact with the 21st Army Group. Corps, having left Paris, had only got a

The American M4A3E8 Sherman medium tank

Weight: 32 tons.
Crew: 5.
Armament: one 76-mm M1A2 gun with 71 rounds, plus one .5-inch M2 and two .3-inch M1919A4 machine guns with 600 and 6,250 rounds respectively.
Armour: hull front 64-mm, sides and rear 38-mm, belly 25-mm, and decking 19-mm; turrent front and sides 64-mm and roof 25-mm.
Engine: one Ford GAA-III inline, 450-hp.
Speed: 30 mph.
Range: 100 miles.
Length: 24 feet 8 inches.
Width: 8 feet 9 inches.
Height: 11 feet $2\frac{7}{8}$ inches.

far as Landrecies. General Bradley, hoping to get Patton out of his supply difficulties, moved it over behind VII Corps and sent it through the Ardennes. On September 9 his 5th Armoured Division (Major-General Lumsford E. Oliver) liberated Luxembourg and, better still, as part of the same advance, crossed the Sûre at Wallendorf (seven miles east of Diekirch) thus making a breach in the Siegfried Line.

At Koblenz, where on September 5 Field-Marshal von Rundstedt had just relieved Model as C.-in-C. West, this news, according to his chief-of-staff Lieutenant-General Westphal, not one inclined to panic, "burst like a bombshell".

"All available forces, all that could be pulled out from other sectors," he added, "were thrown into the breach. Overcoming the most serious hesitations, we went so far as to denude the Trier sector completely. After a week of pitched battles, the enemy went back over the west bank of the Sûre. A gigantic catastrophe was thus averted. If the enemy command had thrown in greater strength at this point,

not only the defensive organisation we were trying to build in the Eifel, but the whole Western Front, which had no reserves worthy of the name, would have crumbled."

This shows that the Koblenz H.Q. had simply no idea of the logistic crisis already affecting the U.S. 7th and 3rd Armies and now extending to the 1st. Nor did they know that Bradley had no reserves with which to exploit Oliver's success. It is true that, according to Westphal, C.-in-C. West's Intelligence service thought that Eisenhower had 60 divisions whereas the figure was actually 50.

The Pas-de-Calais cleared

As his notes of August 17 and 23 show, Montgomery claimed for his reinforced 21st Army Group the distinction of inflicting the final blow on the enemy by a "concentrated push" north of the Ruhr. Yet he had only 18 divisions and six or seven independent brigades, and the

Canadian 1st Army had been given (by him) a job which was to divert it from his ultimate objective. Using six divisions and two brigades, it liberated the ports of Le Havre, Dieppe, Boulogne, Calais, and Dunkirk, captured the V-rocket launching-sites and mopped up the Cape Gris-Nez shore batteries, which used to harass the English coast between North Foreland and Dungeness.

Thus only the British 2nd Army was left to continue the thrust northwards, but by August 30 it had only two of its three corps across the Seine. These had altogether five divisions, including three armoured, two brigades of tanks, and General Piron's Belgian motorised brigade. This was a long way from the "concentrated push" (40 divisions) mentioned the previous week.

Montgomery, usually so cautious towards overweening displays of ill-considered optimism, seems to have yielded to the feeling of euphoria evident at all levels of the Allied high command. And yet the "great encirclement" west of the Seine, for which Patton had been halted in front of Falaise, had not come up to expectations. And, though now reduced to three corps and six divisions, the German 15th Army in the Pas-de-Calais was still a considerable fighting force. On August 23 its new C.-in-C. was Zangen, who took over from Salmuth. Sir Brian Horrocks, C.-in-C. British XXX Corps (11th Armoured, Guards Armoured, and 50th Infantry Divisions and 2nd Armoured Brigade), left the Vernon bridgehead with 600 tanks and made such good progress that 36 hours later his 11th Armoured Division took Amiens by surprise during the night of August 30-31, capturing General Eberbach, who had replaced the wounded Hausser as C.-in-C. 7th Army. The F.F.I. had seized the bridges in the town and the 11th Armoured was thus able to push on to the area of Lens, which it reached on September 11.

On Horrocks's right the Guards, who had crossed the Somme at Bray, were at Douai by nightfall on the same day. On September 3 they were off again and by 1400 hours, having done over 70 miles, got into the outer suburbs of Brussels, accompanied by the Piron brigade, amidst great popular rejoicing. That same evening General Horrocks, who set up his H.Q. in Laeken Park, invited Queen Elisabeth of the Belgians to dinner in his tent.

At the same time 11th Armoured Division had reached Alost and been given the

task of seizing the port of Antwerp to prevent the destruction of its installations. In this it was admirably seconded by the Belgian resistance so that on September 4 its quays (34 miles of them!), docks, and locks, its equipment and the tunnel under the Scheldt all fell intact into Allied hands. In 1960, however, General Horrocks said he thought that the order given to 11th Armoured was a "serious error":

"My excuse is that my eyes were fixed entirely on the Rhine, and everywhere else seemed of subsidiary importance. It never entered my head that the Scheldt would be mined, and that we should not be able to use Antwerp port until the channel had been swept and the Germans cleared from the coastline on either side. Nor did I realise that the Germans would be able to evacuate a large number of the troops trapped in the coastal areas across the mouth of the Scheldt estuary from Breskens to Flushing."

Today it seems that he would have been wiser to order the 11th Armoured Division to by-pass Antwerp and go on across the

△ *Three Canadian gunners inspect one of the 14-inch guns at Boulogne used to bombard the Channel and south coast ports of England. The gun emplacement has a curtain of chain mail, which bears marks of some of the attempts to silence the guns. They stopped firing on September 22 when the garrison commander, Lieutenant-General Heim, surrendered to the Canadians.*

△ ◁ *French civilians start the work of reconstruction. In the background lie the remains of one of the Marne bridges.*

◁ *Two U.S. soldiers put some scanty camouflage on their machine gun nest. When leaves or underbrush were used to conceal a position, care had to be taken to replace them when they wilted, for a heap of yellowing leaves in a green wood was a danger signal to a wise soldier.*

Across the Seine

▬▬▬▬	FRONT LINE ON AUGUST 13
▬▬▬▬	FRONT LINE ON AUGUST 26
▬ ▬ ▬	FRONT LINE ON SEPTEMBER 16
▪×××××▪	BOUNDARY BETWEEN ALLIED ARMY GROUPS
▪××××▪	BOUNDARY BETWEEN ALLIED ARMIES
⬭	GERMAN POCKETS
⬭	GERMAN "FORTRESS"

Amsterdam

The Hague

Arnhem

Rhine

HOLLAND

Vlissingen

Woensdrecht

Zeebrugge

Breskens

Antwerp

Bruges

Ghent

Calais   Dunkirk

Alost

Boulogne

Hasse

Brussels

Liège

Lens

Aix-la-
Chapelle

Béthune

Tournai

Canadian 1st Army

Douai

Mons

BELGIUM

Cambrai

British
2nd Army

Maubeuge

Dieppe

Somme

Bray

Avesnes

Bastogne

Br.
XXX
Corps

Amiens

Le Havre

Montdidier

U.S. 1st Army

Honfleur

Seine

Crozat Canal

Wallendorf

Caen

Rouen

Gournay-en-Bray

Laon

U.S. VII Corps

Br. XII Corps

Louviers

Oise   U.S.
XIX
Corps

Soissons

U.S.
XX Corps

Thionville

Vimoutiers

les Andelys

Rheims

Verdun

Falaise

Nantes

Château
Thierry

Epernay

Saint
Mihiel

Metz

Argentan

Paris

U.S.
XII
Corps

Alençon

Arpajon

Châlons

U.S.
1st Army

U.S. V Corps

Nancy

Fontainebleu

Montereau

Vitry

Commercy

U.S. 3rd Army

Le Mans

Chartres

U.S. XX Corps

Troyes

Neufchâteau

U.S.
XV Corps

U.S. XII Corps

Yonne

Saint
Florentin

Vittel

Beaugency

Joigny

Epinal

Gien

Chaumont

FRANCE

Tours

ELSTER

Landrecies

Albert Canal in one solid mass, then make
for the Woensdrecht isthmus (15 miles
north-east of Antwerp) which has the
only metalled road linking the Zeeland
archipelago to the mainland. This would
have cut off the Germans left behind in
the Scheldt estuary and freed the port
within a few days.

Horrocks must have had in mind the
memoirs of Field-Marshal Montgomery,
published two years earlier, which maintained that the "free use of the port of
Antwerp" was not the only way of bringing the war to a speedy end; it was
necessary at the same time to strike a
"violent decisive blow" against Germany.
It is significant that Horrocks does not
dwell on his former commander's
opinion. Colonel Stacey, the official historian of the Canadian Army, concluded,
as did Horrocks, but in stronger and more
vivid terms: it was "a considerable Allied
misfortune". It would seem that the blame
for this mishap must lie equally with

Montgomery and Eisenhower, as the
latter ordered the British commander on
September 10 to "defer the cleaning out of
the Antwerp approaches" in the interests
of the bridgehead he wanted to get over
the Rhine at Arnhem.

On Horrocks's left Lieutenant-General
Ritchie's XII Corps (7th Armoured and
53rd Infantry Divisions, with 4th Armoured Brigade) avenged its commander's defeats in Libya. Though it had a
harder task, as it was manoeuvring in the
rear of the German 15th Army, it drove
forwards along the axis les Andelys–
Gournay–Saint Pol–Béthune and freed
Ghent on September 5. In the Bruges area
it made contact with the Canadian 1st
Army busy mopping up the Channel ports.

As we can see, General Dempsey had
driven forward at top speed and the
British 2nd Army had equalled the best
records of the American 3rd, though to
get the fuel for XXX and XII Corps, VII
Corps had had to be immobilised.